Embracing God's Future without Forgetting the Past

Embracing God's Future without Forgetting the Past

A Conversation about Loss, Grief, and Nostalgia in Congregational Life

Michael K. Girlinghouse

Fortress Press

Minneapolis

EMBRACING GOD'S FUTURE WITHOUT FORGETTING THE PAST

A Conversation about Loss, Grief, and Nostalgia in Congregational Life

Cover image: © iStock2019 / Vintage White Church by delrick

Cover design: Alisha Lofgren

Print ISBN: 978-1-5064-5888-5

eBook ISBN: 978-1-5064-5889-2

The paper used in this publication meets the minimum requirements of American National Standard for Information Sciences — Permanence of Paper for Printed Library Materials, ANSI Z329.48-1984.

Manufactured in the U.S.A.

To Ann Girlinghouse, my mother,
Who was my first editor when I was a child,
Is my constant supporter,
And shaped the person I am today.

Contents

Acknowledgments

O give thanks to the Lord, for the Lord is good,
    for the Lord's steadfast love endures forever.
(Ps 136:1 paraphrased)

As I think about the journey that has brought this book into being, I am grateful to God for the opportunity to write it and to the many people who have walked with me along the way. At least for me, the writing process has always been a humbling one, hopefully guided by the Holy Spirit. The experience of writing is more like releasing a bird back into the wild than building a house. (I've actually done both.) I never know exactly where I will wind up when I write the first word!

I truly believe that creativity is not so much about thinking something new, but about bringing together the ideas and insights of others in a new way. I have been blessed by the research, study, and thoughts of those who have come before me and whose work fills the pages of the bibliography, and many others who have influenced me over the years. I am grateful for all the students, congregations, and individuals who have taught me so much about life and death, sorrow and hope, faith and discipleship. Many of the experiences I have shared with them are woven into the stories told in this book (though the details have been changed and the stories are compilations).

In addition to the myriad of people and experiences who have influenced me in ways known and unknown, there are some specific people for whom I give thanks. I am extremely grateful to my editor at Fortress Press, Beth Ann Gaede. I appreciate her patience, her advocacy, her creativity, and her many helpful comments and suggestions that made this book so much better; and she did so graciously and in a way that brought the best out of my writing. I am also thankful to Allyce Amidon and to the many others at Fortress who have worked so diligently on bringing this book to life.

I am thankful for my friend and colleague Pastor Liz Albertson, Director of Evangelical Mission in the Arkansas-Oklahoma Synod of the Evangelical Lutheran Church in America. Long before I wrote the first word, Liz and I had many long discussions about many of the ideas that are contained in this book. Her insightful questions pushed me to think deeper about the concepts I was working on, and her keen pastoral sense helped keep me grounded in congregational life and ministry. She took the time to read through the whole manuscript and helped make the content clearer and the conversation boxes more useful. Liz and Ida McAllister, our synod administrative assistant, have forgiven me for being distracted and late in getting things done, and have willingly picked up the slack these past months as I have written and revised the manuscript. What a gift! I am grateful to the Arkansas-Oklahoma Synod Council for granting me the sabbatical leave to write the first draft, and to the whole synod for supporting me and encouraging me in this work.

Words are not enough to share my appreciation and gratitude for my wife, Terrie. She has been my partner in life for the past thirty-six years, walking with me in so many ways. She is the "nonanxious presence" in my life who keeps me from careening off the path, and the voice of quiet wisdom that keeps me grounded. With great forbearance and grace, she has put up with the many hours I spent holed up in my study bent over my laptop. Her compassionate ministry as a wildlife rehabber—nursing birds, turtles, and other creatures back to health and releasing them back into the wild—has taught me a lot about my ministry with congregations and individuals.

Finally, I give thanks for you, the reader, for choosing to read this book. It is my hope and prayer that you find the book useful for thinking about and doing ministry in new ways in changing contexts. If you do, I would encourage you to let others know about it. Where my words have been helpful, I give thanks to the Holy Spirit; where they have not, I take all the blame. May God bless you, your congregation, and Christ's church as, together, we embrace God's future without forgetting our past.

In Christ's Peace,
The Rev. Michael K. Girlinghouse

Preface: Invitation to a Conversation

I will extol you, my God and King
  And bless your name forever and ever. . . .
One generation shall laud your works to another,
  and shall declare your mighty deeds. (Ps 145:1, 4)

I was standing in front of a group of maybe fifteen people in the fellowship hall of their church. Listening. They had gathered for a question-and-response session following worship. Their questions formed an all-too-familiar litany of lament:

"How can we get more young families in our congregation?"

"How can we attract new members?"

"We're getting older, and we just don't have the energy to do things anymore. How can we get others involved?"

"We're getting so small, how will we be able to afford a pastor?"

And finally, the question that summed them all up: "Why can't things be like they used to be?"

Their voices were filled with sadness, anxiety, fear, frustration, and a deep sense of yearning.

As carefully and compassionately as I could, I explained that things would never be like they used to be. The world around them had just changed too much since their congregation's glory days. Families were different. There was a lot more competition for people's time. People just didn't get involved in social organizations anymore. I explained that the church wasn't the only community organization that had declined precipitously since the mid-1960s. A member of the local Lions Club confirmed my claim, and several others nodded in agreement. I pointed out that the emergence of television, the internet, and social media changed the way people engage with one another. I told them that, because of these and many other changes, churches could not hope to re-create the past. What worked in the past simply did not work today.

I used my own experience in campus ministry to prove my point. When I was a student in the early 1980s, simply putting up signs on campus announcing worship times did a pretty good job of attracting students. In those days, our campus ministry at the University of Minnesota had two full services every Sunday. There were always students around our ministry center. People regularly attended other events as well.

By the time I began serving as a campus pastor in 1991, things had changed dramatically. Just putting up signs was not enough to attract participants. In fact, the posters I put up on campus didn't attract anybody. It took months of hard work building relationships and being visible on campus to get the first few students to show up. Serving food was especially useful in attracting participants. We would get ten or fifteen for worship but sometimes as many as sixty for our meals on Sunday evenings, when the college food service was closed.

By the mid-1990s, when I started my second campus ministry, the world had changed again. In those few short years, campuses had changed the way they did food service, and the dining choices for students had multiplied. Evening dinners didn't draw students anymore. They could use their meal cards at the fast-food restaurants downtown when the food service was closed. We couldn't compete. The point was that doing things the way we had always done them—even if we did them bigger and better—simply didn't work. We needed to change. We needed to adapt to what was going on around us.

On top of that, I explained, for Christians, idolizing some past "golden age" was, in fact, heretical. As followers of Jesus Christ, we believe and confess that the fullness of the kingdom of God, though revealed fully in Christ, lies in the future, not the past. To believe that the church reached its peak in the 1950s or '60s or '80s or the 1400s or in the first century seems to deny this core belief.

After I had finished responding, some nodded. Some looked uncertain. Some frowned at the idea of change. All agreed they needed to do something different. They kicked around some ideas. I suggested a few things others were trying. There seemed to be energy in the room. I left feeling hopeful.

Several months later, I visited the congregation again. Nothing had changed. Same litany. Same lament.

Initially, I was frustrated and puzzled by this congregation's inability to step into the future or even begin to imagine what that future might look like. They had all the information. They seemed to understand that changes needed to be made. And then, nothing happened. It wasn't the first time I had experienced this in my work with congregations, but it was still baffling. What, I wondered, was getting in the way of these congregations moving forward? Then, suddenly, it dawned on me: they were not just sad, frustrated, and fearful. They were grieving.

I'm not sure why it didn't occur to me earlier. I taught classes on death, dying, and grief for fifteen years at two universities. Over thirty years of ministry I had provided pastoral care to grieving people of all kinds and in many different circumstances.

As I reflected on this new insight, it occurred to me that this congregation was not only grieving but also exhibiting many of the same signs and symptoms of individuals I had cared for who were "stuck" in their grief—so trapped they could barely function in the present and saw little or no hope for their future.

Like the parents who had not touched a thing in their child's room since the child's death over a year earlier.

Like the widow who curled up on the couch after her husband's death and hadn't really got up for ten years.

Like the man who couldn't bring himself to learn how to cook because the kitchen was his late wife's domain and he felt uncomfortable there.

Like these individuals, the congregation seemed to be so trapped in its yearning for the past that they could not even begin to imagine a new or renewed future, let alone find the energy to take its first steps into that future.

That evening, over five years ago, I wrote the following two questions in my journal: "How does grief and loss affect a social system like a church?" And, "How does that grief and loss manifest itself in nostalgia?"

This book is the result of my search for answers to these two questions. In these pages, I share what I have discovered about how we—as church members, lay leaders, and clergy—can address a congregation's grief over its perceived loss of the past, so we might be freed to embrace God's future for the mission and ministry of Christ's church.

As I began to explore these questions, one of the first things I discovered was that, for a long time, I had been doing it wrong. I should have known better.

In my teaching and pastoral ministry, I have done workshops and made numerous presentations on grief and the grief process and have taught people how to care for those who are grieving. I have lectured on loss and how it affects us. I know that skipping lightly over our grief or trying to skip over it completely to quickly get on with the future is a recipe for all kinds of troubles. I've seen the ill results of attempts to avoid or stuff grief away too many times!

All my study and experience have taught me that one of the *worst* things you can say to a bereaved person is that they should just get over their grief and get on with their lives. I have listened to the intense pain of bereaved parents who have been told they could always have another child, to widows and widowers who have been told they can always get married again, and to people who have been belittled and threatened by employers because they can still barely function a month following a significant death.

I realized that, in effect, I was doing exactly the same thing to this congregation and to others like them who shared their litany of lament with me.

Since that sobering realization, I have changed my approach to congregations that are yearning for their lost glory days. As someone once taught me, "The only way through grief is to grieve." I know from experience that the best way to help someone stuck in their grief is to help them grieve. I have learned that helping a congregation grieve their perceived loss of the past is a much healthier and potentially more effective approach than just encouraging them to "get over" their past to get on with the future. Inviting congregations into a grief process to express the emotions they are feeling about the changes and losses they have experienced, to tell their stories about the joys and sorrows of their past, and to learn how to draw strength from those stories can free them to think more creatively and adaptively about how they can do ministry in the future.

THE EXPERIENCE OF CHANGE

This book is based, in part, on the paradoxical premise that change is a constant in the universe. Change is a part of all of our lives. We are not the same person we were five, ten, or twenty years ago, or even just yesterday. Sometimes we don't even notice it happening. Change can lead to growth or decline. Sometimes change comes to us unannounced and unexpected, while at other times change is the result of conscious choices and the actions we take or fail to take. No matter what the cause of the changes we experience, change almost always results in some kind of loss. We can experience change as something positive or negative in our lives. But, as we will see, even positive changes can result in the experience of loss. We call our reaction to these losses "grief."

Like the congregation in the opening story, many congregations today are dealing with changes that have led to decline and significant loss. While we will discuss some of these changes, this book is not so much about the changes themselves, but about how we work through the experience of loss and the resulting grief those changes generate in us both personally and in the congregational systems of which we are a part.

Since I changed my approach to working with congregations and their litanies of lament, I have become more and more convinced that while yearning for the past can be a barrier to growth in mission and ministry, nostalgic reminiscing can be a tool for adaptive and creative thinking about where God is calling a congregation to go. However, until a congregation comes to terms with its perceived losses from the past through a process of grief, it will continue to be paralyzed in the present and unable to think creatively about the future. Acknowledging and expressing grief will give the congregation the courage to redefine its relationship with the past and draw strength and encouragement from their memories as they step into the future.

AN INVITATION TO A CONVERSATION

I invite you into this conversation about loss, grief, and nostalgia in the life of your congregation and the journey through grief to God's future for your community of faith.

In part 1, we will discuss the nature of loss and grief and present a contemporary, task-based model for understanding the grief process. We will also look at some contemporary ideas about nostalgia and begin to consider how nostalgic feelings can be adaptive. These concepts will give us a common language to use in exploring our experiences of loss and provide a framework for examining the journey from the litany of lament we sing about the loss of our past to engaging ministry in new and renewed ways in the life of the congregation.

Part 2 looks at the impact of loss reflected in the "litany of lament" sung in so many congregations these days. Because each congregation is different, each congregation's experience of loss and grief is different. The part begins with an exercise designed to help you explore your congregation's experience of loss by telling the story of your congregation with the loss left in it. Considering this narrative of growth and decline, joys and sorrows, continuity and change will begin the process of accepting the reality of your losses and expressing the grief you carry because of them.

Setting your congregation's story in the context of the social world in which we find ourselves, the changing trends in religious participation, and shifting understandings of belonging will help you see some of the external factors that have shaped your experience of loss. Examining your congregation as a system that functions much like a family will lead us into a discussion of how your congregation expresses its grief in healthy and unhealthy ways. Part 2 concludes with a chapter that lays out some specific ways you can draw out the grief in your congregation and begin the process of working through that grief. Reflecting on how your congregation currently handles grief and developing processes for expressing grief in healthy ways can allow a community to think more adaptively and creatively about the future.

Part 3 will consider ways your congregation can begin this adaptive and creative work without forgetting or devaluing your past. As the congregation comes to terms with the losses you have experienced and works through the emotions associated with those losses, at some point you will begin looking for ways to more effectively adapt to your present reality. These adaptations will require your congregation to reroot yourselves in Scripture and prayer, redefine your assumptions about being the church, and make adjustments to your life together as a community of faith. We will consider how to meet and overcome challenges to making adaptive changes in the life of the congregation. Using the process of appreciative inquiry, your congregation will be encouraged to draw on nostalgic memories to discover your "positive core," build on your enduring strengths, and consider possible futures.

Part 4 is about embracing God's future for your congregation and making the changes necessary to step into that future. As we work through our grief, we find ourselves more and more emotionally ready to embark on new ways of being church together. Drawing on the strength, courage, and hope from the past, we "remember forward" as we consider God's call to mission and ministry for the congregation. New ways of thinking about ministry require us to learn new skills, develop a new narrative, and allow new patterns of life and relationships to emerge within the congregation. We will look at the variables in a simple formula for understanding how we move from the pain of grief to the first steps toward implementing a new vision, from the sadness of loss to the joy of taking up life again. Because change, with its attending experiences of loss, and grief are constants, your congregation needs to become a learning community that regularly studies Scripture, reflects on the congregation's story, and becomes students of the ever-changing community outside your doors.

I wrote this book with governing boards, such as church councils, committees/teams, and formal and informal church leaders, in mind. Throughout each chapter I offer "In Conversation" questions to ponder and exercises to explore. These are opportunities for you and your group to join the conversation and reflect on your own context, situation, and ministry. At the end of each chapter is a Bible study that will help you connect the themes and main points of the chapter to Scripture. If you are reading the book on your own (without a group for discussion), I encourage you to jot down answers to the "In Conversation" questions and exercises. I hope that, having worked through the book on your own, you will choose to share it with others in your congregation!

A DIFFERENT APPROACH

It is my prayer that by the time you have finished reading this book, you will have worked through your sense of grief and loss and, with a renewed sense of who you are and whose you are, you will feel freed to step out in faith to form new relationships with your neighbors, partner with them in new ministries, and together create new narratives that define you as a community of faith.

Not long ago, I was invited to a congregation to discuss the future of the congregation's ministry. I expected we would be talking about the process for bringing the ministry to a close. The conversation started with the usual litany of lament I've heard many times before.

This time I took a very different approach in responding to their lament. Instead of talking about the necessity of change, or the inevitability (I thought) of their closing, we started by talking about the emotions they felt in the face of the change, loss, and decline they had experienced. The conversation started slowly, but one by one, they began to share their grief and sadness.

Once everyone who wanted to say something had the opportunity to talk, I asked them to tell me about a time when, in their opinion, the congregation was at its best. The mood in the room changed noticeably as they told me stories about their congregation's past.

"What might we learn from those days?" I asked when the storytelling was finished.

"That we need to work together," one man said.

"That you can do a lot with a little," a woman added, remembering the congregation's humble beginnings in another church's basement.

"That, maybe, we can do it again!" a third person offered.

By the time I left several hours later, the conversation had turned to discussing possibilities for new mission and ministry. This congregation may still close. Members may decide that that is exactly what God is calling them to do—and we discussed that too. But they may not. Whatever they decide, I am confident they will feel freed and empowered to act on their decision, and they will do so knowing that God goes with them into whatever the future may hold.

Change is a constant. But God also created us with a sense of continuity—of ourselves as beings with a past, present, and future. This sense of continuity provides stability in our lives, which we need to feel emotionally healthy. We may not be the same person we were ten years ago, but we need to feel connected to that person. We may not know what tomorrow holds, but we anticipate its coming and plan for its approach.

As we face challenges and changes in the present, our yearning for the past can trap us. As we consider our past, we can attempt to re-create it, we can try to forget it, or we can tap into our nostalgic memories in order to learn from it. As we consider the future, we can fear it, try to avoid it, or adapt to the changes that have brought the future to our doorstep. This book shows readers that by acknowledging our losses and working through our grief, we can learn from the past and adapt to changes in the present, so we can embrace God's future with boldness, courage, and hope for the sake of our mission and ministry in Jesus's name.

In the end, this book is not so much about loss, grief, and nostalgia as it is about how we can be freed from grief to creatively adapt and change our ministries to proclaim the gospel in our world today. There are lots of fantastic books out there about how to do ministry effectively in our contemporary culture. But I maintain that in a culture where we avoid death and truncate grief, we need to come to terms with what we have lost before we can even begin to think about how to move forward. My desire—my calling—is to help congregations work through and overcome the barrier of unacknowledged and unresolved grief over the loss of the past. That is the reason I wrote this book.

This is not the last word on these subjects. Not by any stretch. Believing that, I invite you and members of your church into an ongoing conversation about how, in the life of a congregation, we can embrace God's future for us and our congregations without forgetting the past.

Thank you for taking this journey with me.

Peace,
The Rev. Michael K. Girlinghouse

PART I

Leaving Eden: An Introduction to Loss, Grief, and Nostalgia

Therefore the Lord God sent [the man] forth from the garden of Eden. (Gen 3:23)

Carol sat in my office, a box of tissues gripped tightly in her long, thin hands.[1] It had been ten months since her son died in a freak accident while playing with friends. On my recommendation, she had been seeing a counselor to work through her intense grief, but she still stopped by to talk with me from time to time.

"I dusted my son's room the other day," she announced, fighting the tears welling up in her brown eyes.

Up to that point, she had barely been able to go into her son's bedroom. Dusting was a major accomplishment.

"You dusted his room?" I echoed her words, affirming I had heard her, inviting her to say more.

"I was sitting in the living room, flipping through some photo albums, and thinking about what good times we had." She pulled out a tissue and wiped away a tear. "And some of the not so good ones." She laughed weakly. "There was a picture of him standing in the living room covered with mud. I remember yelling at him . . . and then grabbing the camera." She paused for a moment, a wistful look on her face. Then she continued, "When I got to the end of the album I just knew it was time. My counselor kept telling me I would know when the time was right, and I did. I cried the whole time."

Loss, grief, and nostalgia are common human experiences. All three have been shown to transcend the boundaries of culture, ethnicity, religion, social status, and language. Starting with the story of the expulsion from the garden of Eden, loss, and a yearning to return to a time of perfection before the loss, play a role in many of the stories of the Bible. Stories of loss and yearning play a role in many other religious traditions as well. A remarkable similarity in nostalgic thinking has been documented and studied in places as diverse as the United States, China, and Ethiopia, as well as in many other nations and cultures.[2] Loss, grief, and nostalgia can touch our lives from the earliest days of childhood to our elder years. But while it is true that these are basic human experiences, it is surprising how little time most of us spend reflecting on them. Instead, most people simply accept them, unexamined, as part of human life, or worse, do their best to avoid their impact and meaning altogether. Much of what is said, taught, and believed in Western popular culture about loss, grief, and nostalgia is either vastly oversimplified, based on outdated ideas, or just plain wrong.

Because of these common misunderstandings, before we begin looking at how loss, grief, and nostalgia can impact a congregation as it thinks about its future mission and ministry, we need to lay out some basic principles and concepts about these three common, often related, and frequently misconstrued experiences in human life. This overview will ground our discussion in contemporary thinking about these subjects and give us a shared framework and language for our conversations.

Research on grief has primarily focused on individuals and their response to the death of a loved one or other significant relationships. In recent years, this work has been expanded to consider how grief results from other kinds of loss and the ways it influences family systems. This overview will largely focus on these bodies of work and begin to apply those insights to the experience of loss in congregations.

Contemporary research about nostalgia has challenged some of our common assumptions about our human tendency to reminisce about the past. This work, too, has focused on the experience of individuals but can be applied to our communal reminiscing. As we consider how congregations think about the past, we will reconsider how helpful nostalgic thinking can be as a congregation contemplates its future.

1

Empty Places: The Experience of Loss

Which one of you, having a hundred sheep and losing one of
them, does not leave the ninety-nine in the wilderness and go
after the one that is lost until he finds it? (Luke 15:4)

Whether we remember it or not, all of us have experienced
loss. Loss can leave an empty place in our hearts longing to be
filled. Like Carol in our opening story, we sometimes experience losses that are significant and have a profound effect
on our lives. Other times, the losses we experience are minor,
barely grieved and only vaguely remembered. The empty
pocket that once held your wallet may be fairly easy to fill,
but the empty chair at Christmas dinner that belonged to a
deceased loved one may never be. Some have argued that loss
is the very first thing we experience in life as we leave the
comfort of our mother's womb and enter the wider world
during the trauma of birth. Losses come in all shapes and sizes.
As we will discover, some losses are not easily recognized as
losses. Some losses come as the result of other losses, losses
piled upon losses. Losses come as we pass through devel-

opmental stages, deal with the realities of aging bodies and minds, and experience changes in roles and relationships in our unfolding lives.

In Conversation

Think about the losses you have experienced over the course of your life. After a few minutes of reflection, make a list. Don't think about just the "big" losses, but the little ones as well.

- Look back over your list. How did these losses make you feel? Sad? Angry? Frustrated? Glad?
- In your group, share some of your experiences of loss with one another.
- Did others' experiences remind you of losses you had forgotten?
- Could you relate your experience of loss to theirs?
- Were your feelings similar or different?

A loss—whether big or small—is always experienced as a deprivation, a separation from that which is lost.[1] We had something, and now we don't. We feel deprived of whatever that person, object, or status provided for us, whether that was comfort or clout or companionship. That loss is experienced as deprivation may seem obvious, but it is this characteristic of loss that generates the emotional response and other reactions we call "grief."[2] When we lose something, our relationship or attachment to that thing is severed, and we feel that. The deprivation we feel can be as tangible as not being able to access our house or start our car because we lost our keys, or considerably less tangible, like losing our role as a husband or wife due to death or a divorce, or losing the status that came with the job we just lost, or losing our connection to the past.

It is important to note that loss does not always come as the result of negative experiences. Losses can be experienced in positive settings and circumstances too. For example, for most people, graduation from high school is a positive experience, one people work hard to accomplish and look forward to achieving. There are many positive emotions associated with graduation: joy, relief, a sense of fulfillment, freedom, and maturity. But there are also losses associated with graduation and leaving high school. I had friends in high school I haven't seen since graduation day and probably never will. We leave behind the familiar routine of a structured school day for whatever life after high school brings. In the transition to work, school, volunteer or military service, or whatever lies ahead, the roles that defined us in high school are lost or significantly changed.

The experience of separation and deprivation that comes with loss always initiates some kind of grief response within us. The greater and more complex the sense of deprivation, the deeper and more complicated the grief. Grief is always directly related to the level and nature of the relationship we have with what we have lost. That is why no two grief experiences are ever the same. Losing one's keys may cause us a few moments of grief. The grief Carol experienced when her son died is likely to last the rest of her life. Every time she passes what would have been a milestone in the child's life, she will likely grieve his loss again. In the same way, two people experiencing the same loss may have very different responses to that loss.

In addition, each person's relationship with what was lost is almost certainly different simply because the people experiencing the loss are different. Going back to our example from high school graduation, we can see that some individuals work through the losses associated with graduation with relative ease while others struggle mightily with them as they make the transition to whatever is next. Someone who has no idea what is coming after graduation may find it harder to make the transition than a classmate who has a full-ride scholarship to a university. A person who had significant leadership roles in athletics or student government may find leaving those roles behind more difficult than someone who was bullied by their peers.

As we begin to discuss how a congregation responds to a perceived loss of its past, remembering that not all people will experience the congregation's losses in the same way will be important. The complexity of a congregation's response to loss is directly related to the nature of the loss and the diversity of the people who participate at various levels in the congregation's life.

Our experiences of loss over our lifetime shape us as individuals and as communities. Smaller losses can prepare us to face bigger losses in the future. The way we worked through a previous loss can inform our response to a subsequent loss, sometimes in ways of which we are completely unaware. These experiences are cumulative in their effect. Multiple losses over a short period of time can be difficult to handle. Each relationship lost must be grieved separately, but this can be very difficult to sort out. This is one of the reasons the grief following a tragedy or disaster can be so difficult to work through. People experiencing multiple losses in a year almost always need a counselor or therapist to help with their grief. The same is true for congregations that are dealing with multiple losses. Unresolved grief from previous losses can be carried over into the current experience of loss.

Sam, a student in one of my courses on death and dying, told the class the story of losing the family dog when he was a child. He was in early elementary school when, one afternoon, he came home to find his beloved dog missing. "Spot went to live someplace else," his mother told him without looking up from what she was doing. Sam was shocked. He felt betrayed, angry, hurt, and sad. He asked his mother where the dog had gone. He wanted to get her back. His mother was, at best, evasive. A few weeks later, the family got a new puppy, and Spot was never mentioned again, though Sam always carried the sense of hurt and betrayal with him.

Many years later, Sam found out that Spot had been killed on the road and hastily buried prior to Sam coming home from school. His parents agreed to tell their child that Spot had gone to live someplace else to save him from having to deal with the death of his pet. As it turned out, their good intentions taught Sam an unfortunate lesson about loss that he never forgot. That lesson was reinforced in a family system that rarely dealt with losses directly, preferring to bury them quickly with a minimum of emotion or comment.

Sam took my class because he was struggling with the death of his grandmother, with whom he had been very close. What he had learned about dealing with loss wasn't working. His relationship with his grandmother could not be easily swept aside. His feelings of betrayal, hurt, and anger were difficult to understand and generated a lot of guilt. Working with a counselor helped him to connect the dots and learn how his previous experiences of loss affected his response to his grandmother's death.

Not all the lessons we learn from our experiences of loss are this profound or significant. Even much less significant losses can teach us life lessons.

When I was maybe nine or ten, I lost my wallet as I rode my bike home from the local swimming pool. I didn't have a lot in the wallet except my pool pass. But losing it was a big deal, because, in my ten-year-old mind, it meant not being able to go to the pool the rest of the summer. My mom had me ride back over my course to see if I could find it. She told me to check at the pool. Maybe I had left it in the changing room. I hunted and hunted but never found the wallet. We did buy a replacement pass, but my mom made me pay something toward it from my weekly allowance. (I think my

9

allowance was a quarter at the time.) Having to contribute to the new pass made an impression on me. I think the only reason I remember that experience of loss from my childhood is the lesson I learned about being responsible and taking responsibility. That lesson stays with me to this day.

In Conversation

Think back to your own experiences of loss.

- How did those around you react to the loss?
- How did they support you as you reacted to it?
- What messages did they give you about loss and how we should cope with it?

Whether you knew it or not, each one of those experiences was a learning opportunity for you.

- What did you learn?
- Looking back, how do you think your early experiences of loss shaped later experiences?

SYMBOLIC LOSSES

As you can see from these examples, loss comes to us in a variety of ways. Many of the losses we experience involve tangible things that we can point to: possessions, people, and places. But these tangible, physical losses often result in secondary, symbolic losses that involve the loss of roles, relationships, and status. We call these losses "secondary" not because they are less important, but because they come as a result of another loss. On the contrary, these losses may be more significant and have a greater impact on our lives than the loss that originally caused them. Secondary, symbolic losses are often more difficult to identify and recognize than physical, tangible ones. They may not even be recognized as losses that need to be acknowledged and worked through.[3] But even if

10

they are not recognized, they can touch us deeply, affecting our social status, sense of self, spiritual beliefs, and values.

Symbolic losses are often grieved longer than physical losses. For example, Bill loses his job as an emergency room nurse due to layoffs. Eventually, he finds a new position working for a doctor in a local clinic. He is happy with his new job, but sometime later he finds he is still struggling with sadness and a yearning for his previous position. He can't understand why he is having these feelings until, with the help of a counselor, he realizes the change in job is about more than a shift in the way he makes a living.

Bill's experience of being laid off comes with layers of losses, each producing its own responses and reactions. The primary level of loss, being temporarily deprived of his livelihood, will bring one set of responses and reactions. At the next level, moving from the crisis-focused world of the emergency room to the more routine work of a local clinic represents a change in role and a loss of identity as he redefines what it means to be a nurse. At an even deeper level, his experience of being laid off could generate feelings of rejection that affect his sense of personal value and result in the loss of self-worth. At first, Bill did not even recognize the effect all these changes had on his sense of self. Can you think of other secondary and symbolic losses that might have resulted from Bill losing his job?

In Conversation

Look back at your list of losses and select one to focus on for this conversation.

- Think about the losses Bill experienced. Can you identify some of the secondary and symbolic losses you experienced? Consider losses of status, relationships, and roles.
- How did these losses affect your sense of self?
- How were assumptions about your world challenged or changed by these losses?
- Share your thoughts with your group.
- Discuss how identifying secondary, symbolic losses can help us better understand our responses and reactions to the losses we experience.

Because symbolic losses affect us at a deeper level, the ramifications can often reach much further than physical losses. A person whose spouse dies may face significant changes in their social status as they move from "husband" or "wife" to "widow" or "widower." No longer part of a "couple," bereaved spouses often find other couples stepping away from them. A debilitating injury or illness can have long-term effects on relationships, roles, and self-esteem. A long-term illness can require rearranging roles in the household as other family members pick up tasks done by the person who is ill, and lead to the person feeling useless or a burden. A move to a new town or city can open up opportunities to redefine one's self, explore new roles, and abandon unhealthy lifestyles or habits.

LOSS IN CONGREGATIONAL LIFE

Like individuals, congregations can experience loss and the impact of loss in a variety of ways and at many levels. The departure of members because of relocation, conflict, or death can result in the loss of their friendship, their leadership, and their gifts, skills, and financial support. Fires, disasters, robbery, and vandalism can result in the loss of possessions, including the church building itself. Trauma, crisis, or violence in the broader community can lead to a loss of security and safety. Pastors and other staff members and leaders leave, and the congregation may experience multiple losses that are complex and difficult to deal with, resulting in the congregation's carrying a significant amount of unresolved grief.

In addition to the losses experienced in the history of the congregation, a congregation's experience of loss is made even more complex because each individual member, visitor, or friend brings with them experiences of loss from their personal lives and previous congregations. Intentionally or unintentionally, aware or unaware, a congregation reacts and responds to all these layers of loss.

Considering the wide range of losses a congregation may need to work through is outside the scope of this book. Here, I want to look specifically at a congregation's perceived loss of the past, of the "glory days" when the congregation was at its finest and best. I say "perceived" loss of the past, because that "lost" past will be defined, remembered, and grieved differently by different individuals and groups within the congregation. Longtime members and newcomers may have very different perspectives on when the "glory days" of the congregation were. Individuals will assign different levels of significance to various losses as they think about days gone by. One member may find a loss weighing heavily on their heart, while another barely notices it occurred. The intersection of these varying perspectives will shape the way the congregation thinks about, talks about, and considers the past as they look to the future of the congregation's ministry.

All losses result in some level of grief response. These responses can be as complex and varied as the losses that produced them. Still, there is a lot we can say, in general, about

13

how we experience grief and work through the broad range of reactions commonly generated by loss.

BIBLE STUDY: LUKE 15:1–32

In Luke 15:1–32, Jesus tells parables about a lost sheep, a lost coin, and a lost son.

1. Have someone in your group read Luke 15:1–32 aloud. Have the reader pause for a moment between each parable to give time for reflection.

2. Think about each parable from the perspective of what we have been learning about loss.

   • What is the primary loss the shepherd, the woman, and the father experienced?

   • What secondary, symbolic losses might they have experienced? How might these secondary losses have affected them?

3. Jesus tells these parables in response to the Pharisees and scribes grumbling about his welcome to tax collectors and sinners (v. 2).

   • Reflect on the primary and secondary losses experienced by the sheep, the coin (use your imagination), and the son. How might these losses have affected them?

   • What is Jesus trying to teach the Pharisees and scribes about loss and welcoming the lost?

   • What might Jesus be trying to teach *us* about facing our own losses and welcoming the lost into our congregations?

A Twisting Road: The Journey of Grief

But we do not want you to be uninformed, brothers and sisters, about those who have died, so that you may not grieve as others do who have no hope. (1 Thess 4:13)

Grief is more than just an emotional response to the experience of loss. It can manifest itself physically, psychologically, behaviorally, and spiritually. Grief is a reaction to loss that is expressed both internally—in our hearts, minds, and souls, and externally—in and through our relationships and interactions with family, friends, and strangers.

Physical reactions to grief can include loss of appetite, headache, hollowness in the stomach, abdominal pain, tightness or a weight in the chest, a lump in the throat, sighing, weakness, lack of energy, insomnia, and, of course, tears.

Psychological reactions include feelings of yearning, sadness, remorse, regret, relief, guilt, anger, shame, anxiety, loneliness, anguish, abandonment, fear, joy, depression, irritation, acceptance, and many others. Thoughts of disbelief, confusion, preoccupation, lack of concentration, and even suicidal thoughts may be a part of grief.

✓ *Behavioral reactions* such as social withdrawal, loss of interest in life activities, avoidance, searching for what was lost, restlessness, problems in interpersonal relationships, the inability to function within an organization or workplace, lashing out, blaming, and transference of feelings can all be expressions of grief.

✓ *Spiritual reactions* can manifest themselves in both religious and nonreligious ways. Grief can lead us to question the meaning and purpose of our lives, reexamine or change our values, or question or lose our faith in God. In our grief we can find ourselves blaming God and distancing ourselves from our faith community. Grief can also drive us deeper into familiar spiritual disciplines or lead us to adopt new spiritual practices, beliefs, and commitments.[1]

GRIEF AND FAITH

Grief is the normal and expected reaction to a loss. As we saw in chapter 1, grief is the natural reaction to the separation and deprivation that come with loss. But not everyone understands grief this way. More than once, I have provided pastoral care to Christians who have questioned their own faith and felt ashamed because they were grieving. Their thinking typically goes something like this: "If I truly believe my loved one is in heaven and believe that someday I will join them there, I shouldn't feel so bad about their death. I should feel happy for them. But I don't. There must be something wrong with my faith." The problem with this line of thinking is that, even if we anticipate a joyful reunion in the afterlife, the separation caused by death and other losses is still real. And it hurts.

Both the Hebrew and Christian Scriptures acknowledge the reality of loss and the legitimacy of the grief that loss brings, even to people of faith. The Scriptures teach that, while faith does not eliminate grief, it helps us face grief, cope with it, and work our way through it.

The Psalms feature many laments expressing the emotions of grief in the face of sickness, death, defeat, and loss. Psalm 137, which mourns the destruction of Jerusalem at the time of the Babylonian exile, begins,

> By the rivers of Babylon—
>> there we sat down and there we wept
>> when we remembered Zion.

The opening verses of Psalm 22, which Jesus cries out from the cross, powerfully expresses the pain of loss and the depth of human grief.

> My God, my God, why have you forsaken me?
>> Why are you so far from helping me, from the words of my groaning?
> O my God, I cry by day, but you do not answer;
>> and by night, but find no rest.

The prophets grieve for their people even as they declare God's judgment against them. Isaiah declares to Judah,

> Therefore I said:
> Look away from me,
>> let me weep bitter tears;
> do not try to comfort me
>> for the destruction of my beloved people. (22:4)

And Jeremiah proclaims,

Give glory to the Lord your God
> before he brings darkness,
and before your feet stumble
> on the mountains at twilight;
while you look for light,
> he turns it into gloom
> and makes it deep darkness.
But if you will not listen,
> my soul will weep in secret for your pride;
my eyes will weep bitterly and run down with tears,
> because the Lord's flock has been taken captive. (13:16–17)

Even Jesus expressed grief and sorrow with tears when his friend Lazarus died, even knowing that he would raise him from the grave (John 11:35).

The hope of Easter and the promise of eternal life help us to face grief, not avoid it. Paul affirmed this hope to the church in Thessalonica as they faced persecution for their faith: "But we do not want you to be uninformed, brothers and sisters, about those who have died, so that you may not grieve as others do who have no hope" (1 Thess 4:13).

People of faith do grieve, and the expression of grief is supported by Scripture, but the common belief that faith precludes grief supports, or perhaps grows from, the propensity of popular American culture to deny death and avoid grief.

GRIEF IN AMERICAN CULTURE

Grief may be normal and expected in the face of loss, but in American mainstream culture, the expression of grief is often limited, dampened, avoided, or ignored. Even in the face of a significant death, individuals are culturally expected to return to normal activities and functioning within a few weeks after the funeral or memorial service. Over the past century and a half, mourning customs have become more and more truncated, to the point where brief memorial services have become almost as common as funerals in many places. According to the National Funeral Directors Association (NFDA), in 2018 the cremation rate in the United States was expected to exceed burials, and the majority of those cremated will not have a traditional funeral with a casket, viewing, and formal service. The NFDA reports that, in 2016, just over 25 percent of those cremated had this kind of traditional funeral.[2]

In America's "death-defying" culture—where death is often presented and perceived as a defeat or a failure, and in spite of the many volumes written about death, dying, and grief in the past fifty years—expressing our grief beyond the memorial service has increasingly become taboo. Anthropologist Margaret Mead is reported to have said of American mourning practices, "When a person is born, we rejoice, and when they are married, we jubilate, but when we die, we try to pretend nothing happened."[3] Few, if any, of the formal rituals, customs, or practices that traditionally followed a funeral or memorial service have survived into the twenty-first century. Since the massive death and disruption of the Civil War, rituals following a death like wearing mourning clothes, marking the doors of the house, visiting the bereaved, holding events to mark the anniversary of the death, and other customs have gradually disappeared. Even practices like bringing food to the bereaved family for weeks following the funeral have diminished, especially in urban and suburban communities.

Because of this movement within American culture toward avoiding grief and limiting our expressions of it, our experience with and understanding of this normal and expected process has also become limited.

CHANGING IDEAS ABOUT GRIEF

Our understanding of the grief process is also held captive by the "stages of grief" identified by Elisabeth Kübler-Ross in her 1970 book, *On Death and Dying*.[4] Kübler-Ross's original research was done with a relatively small sample of terminally ill patients as they related their experience of grief as they mourned their own death. Her work was later applied to grief in general. Many people can name Kübler-Ross's stages: denial, anger, bargaining, depression, and acceptance. For fifty years, Kübler-Ross's stage theory has been used by scholars, filmmakers, authors, preachers, and people on the street to describe the experience of grief as if it were the last word spoken on the subject. The truth is, to talk about grief from this perspective is like discussing the use of communication technology in the church today as if cell phones were never invented and we were still using touch-tone phones (which were introduced in 1963).

While Kübler-Ross was a pioneer in the field of thanatology (the study of death and dying), much has been learned about grief since her seminal work. At best, she identified five common emotions people experience as they go through the process of grief, but she was a long way from describing the fullness of what it means to grieve. Kübler-Ross herself acknowledges in her book that not everyone goes through the stages in the order she presents and that not everyone experiences all five emotions as they grieve.[5] The other problem with this approach to grief is that for many people, the "stage theory," which was meant to be descriptive, has become prescriptive. Popular use has reduced what is a complex experience to a simple formula that does not correspond well to what most people actually go through as they mourn.

Rather than following stages or steps, most people find that grief is a nonlinear journey that twists and turns and folds back on itself even as it moves forward in halting, jerky steps toward resolution. For most people grief feels more like traveling a winding mountain road without guardrails than flying along at eighty miles per hour across the prairie on a straight-as-an-arrow Midwestern interstate.

CONTEMPORARY UNDERSTANDINGS OF GRIEF

Contemporary understandings of grieving and the grief process have moved away from talking about "stages" to more dynamic, task-based models that more adequately describe the complex responses and reactions that occur when we experience loss.

One model, presented by psychologist Therese Rando, identifies the "six Rs" that describe the tasks one must work through to resolve their grief:

1. *Recognize* the loss (acknowledge and understand the death).

2. *React* to the separation (experience the pain; feel, identify, accept, and express the reaction to the loss; identify and mourn secondary losses).

3. *Recollect and reexperience* the deceased and the relationship (review and remember realistically, revive and reexperience the feelings from the relationship).

4. *Relinquish* the old attachments to the deceased and the old assumptive world (surrender attachments to assumptions about the world and oneself based on the relationship and previous experience with the deceased).

5. *Readjust* to move adaptively into the new world without forgetting the old (develop a new relationship with the deceased, adopt new ways of being in the world and form a new identity).

21

6. *Reinvest* (emotional energy from the previous relationship in new relationships).[6]

While Rando's model still presents something of a progression from the initial experience of loss to the resolution of grief, she makes it clear that the tasks are not consecutive "steps" or "stages." Tasks can be worked on concurrently or consecutively. They may be revisited and repeated along the way as circumstances and situations change. Tasks may even resurface years after the grief has been "resolved" due to new experiences of loss, life events, or unexpected reminders of the person who died.

CONTINUING BONDS

Like Rando's model, the majority of task-based models assume that grief is a process that helps us to cope with a loss and sever our attachments to that which was lost. This concept of "grief work" dates back to Sigmund Freud's 1917 paper "Mourning and Melancholia," where Freud argues that the purpose of mourning is to withdraw our emotional attachments to the object that is lost.[7] Freud goes on to say that we never willingly abandon our emotional attachments to what has been lost. This unwillingness results in an emotional struggle between our desire to hold onto those attachments and letting them go. Grief is resolved when an individual overcomes that struggle, relinquishes emotional attachments, and realizes that it is better to "let go" of their bonds to the deceased than to continue holding onto them.

Since the mid-1990s, our understanding of the purpose of grief and grief work has shifted from "letting go" of our bonds to the deceased to redefining our continuing bonds with the one we have lost.[8] Grief work is no longer understood to be about severing attachments, but is viewed as a process through which we move from a "lived," physical rela-

22

tionship with the person who has died to a relationship of memory. According to psychologist William Worden, grief work enables us to find "an enduring connection with the deceased in the midst of embarking on a new life."[9] It is about learning how to realistically remember the person and the part they played in your life, while still moving on with your life by investing renewed energy in continuing and new relationships.

While the focus of our grief work will change and the intensity lessen over time, because we continue to carry these memories with us, our grief never fully ends. The only way grief would ever truly end is if we were to completely forget the person we have lost, and we probably couldn't do that even if we wanted to. While these bonds of remembering continue, grief work will take us to a place where we understand in a deep and visceral way that we cannot put life back the "way things were," before the loss, that things will never be the way they used to be, and that we have begun to adapt to the new reality and live into it.

WILLIAM WORDEN'S TASK-BASED MODEL

Worden's model for describing the grief process and the purpose of grief work identifies four tasks:

1. to accept the reality of the loss,

2. to process the pain of grief,

3. to adjust to the world without the deceased, and

4. to find an enduring connection with the deceased in the midst of embarking on a new life.[10]

Over the years, I have found Worden's model to be extremely beneficial to the grieving people I have cared for and as I have reflected on my own experiences of grief. In explaining the grief process to mourners, Worden's model has helped me explain grief in a way that is both simple to grasp and clearly describes the complexity of most people's experience. While the four tasks can be separated for the purpose of discussion, in reality, the tasks overlap, and inform and relate to each other as the mourner sorts through the physical, emotional, behavioral, and spiritual reactions of their grief. While most mourners tend to focus on the tasks in the order they are presented, in truth, they are all present throughout the grief process. A widow who has to move shortly following the death of a spouse may have to quickly adjust to the changed reality (task 3), even as she tries to accept the fact that her husband is gone (task 1). The parent whose child has died may have to work through the pain of their grief (task 2) all over again when the day the child would have graduated from high school comes, even though they had long since relocated their relationship to their child to one of memory (task 4).

Another advantage of Worden's model is that the most recent edition of his seminal work, *Grief Counseling and Grief Therapy: A Handbook for the Mental Health Practitioner*, has been updated to take into account some of the newer understandings of grief and the purpose of the grief process. While I will be drawing insights from Rando's model of the grief process, I will primarily be using Worden's tasks to structure our conversation as we consider how congregations deal with their perceived loss of the past. Let's look at each of Worden's tasks in turn.

TASK 1. TO ACCEPT THE REALITY
OF THE LOSS

When our life is interrupted by a significant loss, our first reaction is often shock and disbelief. This initial grief response is a coping mechanism that protects us from the wave of emotions that crash over us when facing a loss and numbs us to the pain of the separation we are experiencing. Even when a loss is anticipated, a certain amount of shock and disbelief often accompanies the reality of the actual loss.

Kübler-Ross identified "denial" as the first stage of grieving and "acceptance" as the final stage. In truth, denial and acceptance lace themselves throughout the grief process, performing a dance as we work through the myriad reactions and responses to the loss that descend on us in the days, weeks, months, and even years after a loss.

The first task of grieving is to "get our head around" the reality of the loss we have suffered. At first, we may deny the facts of the loss, especially if the cause of the loss was unclear. We want to know why this loss happened to us. We search for reasons but cannot find a satisfying answer. We assign blame, sometimes illegitimately. We keep expecting our keys to turn back up. We try to convince ourselves that the tornado that destroyed our home was just a dream. We tell ourselves that the person is not really dead and create stories to explain why the person is no longer there. Little by little, we begin to accept the fact that what we had is lost and is not coming back. While we might quickly be able to articulate our loss on an intellectual level, accepting the reality of a loss on an emotional level may take quite a bit longer.

As the days and weeks unfold, and we begin to cope with symbolic and secondary losses, we may begin to deny the meaning of the loss. We tell ourselves that life will go on as usual. We believe we can put things right and restore things to the way they used to be. The boss will call and offer us our job back. We will rebuild the house exactly as it was before the fire. The widower convinces himself that his "couple friends" don't call anymore because they are just busy. Accepting the ongoing ramifications, changed meanings, and altered life-patterns can take even more effort than acknowledging the initial loss.

We can find ourselves having to rework task 1 even years after a loss. More than once, I've had to do it myself. Here are two short examples from my own life.

It has been over twenty-five years since I experienced a devastating fire in the church where I served. Still, I occasionally reach to my bookshelf for a book that was destroyed by the fire. When I do that, I have to accept the reality of that loss all over again.

One Christmas, ten years after my father died, I was walking through a crowded mall and, in the melee, saw a tall, white-haired man several feet in front of me. I took a step toward him, wondering why my father was at the mall. The feeling passed almost as quickly as it came. But, in that instant, I had to revisit task 1.

Acceptance of the reality of the loss comes as we are confronted again and again with the absence of what we have lost and are forced to acknowledge that absence.[11] In the early days following a death or other loss, the bereaved person is frequently asked and is happy to share a response to the question, "What happened?" This recital of events helps to break through the denial and begins to break down the surreal feeling of the loss. At some point, the bereaved person tires of repeating the story, which is a sign that, for the moment anyway, they have worked through task 1. Emotional acceptance comes as they do the work of Worden's second task.

TASK 2. TO PROCESS THE PAIN OF GRIEF

Because, as we have discussed, most Western cultural mourning customs have disappeared, and American popular culture encourages us to get over our grief quickly, the barriers to working on Worden's second task are many. Because grief is often driven underground, it has a way of reemerging in unhealthy and destructive ways. People use alcohol and drugs to mitigate the emotional pain of a significant loss. Unresolved grief can lead to physical sickness and even death.

But, as I have said, the only way through grief is to grieve. At some point, we need to confront the pain of separation and deprivation that inevitably comes from loss. Avoiding it does not make it go away; it only kicks it down the road, bottles it up inside, or squeezes it out in unhelpful and sometimes hurtful ways.

Like the dance of denial and acceptance, the pain of grief can come and go in varying intensities throughout the grief process. Unfortunately, for most people the pain of grief doesn't set in until after the funeral is over, the guests have departed, and the mourner is expected to be back to their daily routines of work, school, child care, or volunteer activities. After a disaster, the numbness of grief wears off just about the time the TV cameras and horde of helpful volunteers disappear, leaving the victims standing alone with their pain in a pile of rubble and ash. The pain can sneak up on you months after a loss, when you least expect it, triggered by a sight, a sound, a smell, or a familiar place.

I was having lunch with an older parishioner at a local restaurant when suddenly, he got tears in his eyes. I asked what was happening. A bit embarrassed, he wiped his eyes and said, "The meal you just ordered was one of my wife's favorites." It had been years since she had died, we had eaten at the restaurant together before, and I had ordered the same dish with no effect. But this time, my order touched something that brought the man's grief to the surface.

Though few if any mourning rituals remain in our society, there are still ways for us to deal constructively with the pain of our grief. Sharing stories and memories of a lost loved one or other devastating loss with a friend, loved one, or other safe person can be very helpful. Creating new rituals, strategies, and traditions to mark birthdays, anniversaries, holidays, and other special occasions can help you express your feelings around those vulnerable times. Having a safe place to express your emotions in constructive ways is important. Working with a counselor, therapist, pastor, or other religious professional can help sort out questions of faith, theology, and meaning. Joining a grief support group can connect you with people who will understand what you are going through. Exercising, meditating, praying, eating a healthy diet, and getting adequate sleep can all contribute to working through the pain of a loss.

TASK 3. TO ADJUST TO THE WORLD WITHOUT THE DECEASED

Over time, a grieving person will begin to adjust to the fact that whatever is lost is gone and is not coming back. Loss is not a problem to be solved; it is a reality to which we need to adapt. We can rebuild the house that was destroyed by fire, but it won't be the same as the one that burned. We can find another job, even in our field, but the relationships with colleagues and customers will be different. We can remarry after the death of a spouse, but to do so thinking the new spouse will replace the deceased spouse is a formula for divorce and further pain. We cannot replace our parents, or a child who died, or a friendship that is lost. Instead, as I have said, the purpose of grief work is to slowly learn how to live in a world without whatever it is we have lost, with all that might mean.

[handwritten: 5 The building during construction.]

As the bereaved person begins to reengage the world around them, external, internal, and spiritual adjustments need to be made.[12] Like the work of the other tasks, these adjustments begin early in the grief process and continue throughout. The first adjustments we have to make are usually external. These include all the ways a loss affects our everyday functioning. I have arranged help for bereaved spouses who needed to learn how to cook, do the laundry, balance a checkbook, and put gas in the car. After a divorce, new living arrangements need to be worked out. In a disaster, meeting basic survival needs becomes an immediate concern. But over time, more subtle and long-term external adjustments must be made. Shifts in roles and relationships need to be dealt with; changes in family habits, rituals, and routines will need to be negotiated; sometimes decisions will need to be made about living arrangements, possessions, and personal items. These adjustments can result in further losses that will also need to be grieved. *[handwritten: Changes, challenges we've met! Can't we be done?]*

Internal adjustments will also need to be made. How we think of ourselves will change as we deal with a loss. According to Worden, a loss can fundamentally affect our self-definition, self-esteem, and sense of self-efficacy.[13] In the case of the death of a spouse, or a divorce, thinking of ourselves as single rather than married can take some adjustment. Dealing with the psychological stress of being victimized in a robbery or violent crime can take time and effort. Facing a loss can often leave us feeling out of control and overwhelmed. Addressing feelings of guilt and shame, whether legitimate or not, may require the help of a counselor or therapist.

Working through some losses will force us to reexamine and adjust our beliefs, worldview, values, and assumptions about life. These spiritual adjustments can challenge the core of who we are and can be the most difficult to make. In her book on the psychology of trauma, psychology professor

29

Ronnie Janoff-Bulman identifies several assumptions that a traumatic loss can challenge, including that the world is a benevolent, safe, and secure place; that the world is meaningful, just, and fair; and that we can control what happens to us by our behavior.[14] After a loss, our basic sense of trust can be shattered. That trust can be rebuilt, but our beliefs about the world around us will never be the same. Adapting to this new way of seeing the world can take a long, long time.

Spiritual adjustments to a significant loss can also include addressing religious questions and concerns. Those who believe in an all-powerful and all-loving God can wrestle with the question of why evil exists in the world when faced with a tragedy, trauma, or death. Rabbi Harold Kushner's 1981 book, *When Bad Things Happen to Good People*, which addressed these questions for a popular audience, was an international best seller. These questions can crush a person's faith, and fill a person with doubt about the very existence of God.

I met Aaron many years ago in one of my classes. He had taken the class because of the sudden death of a close friend. After the first class period, where I told the class that I was a pastor (I always did), he approached me.

"So, you're a pastor, right?" There was challenge in his voice.

I nodded.

"Well, I just want you to know that I don't believe in God anymore." His anger boiled just below the surface.

"Why do you say that?" I asked as nondefensively as I could.

He went on to tell me about his friend's death and the deep spiritual questions it had raised for him.

Our after-class conversations continued off and on throughout the semester. Toward the end of the term, he approached me with a sheepish grin on his face.

"What's up?" I asked.

"I decided that I must believe in God," he announced.

"Really? Why the change?"

He shrugged. "I decided I couldn't be this angry at someone I didn't believe in."

Aaron was in the process of making the spiritual adjustments that are often a part of task 3.

[handwritten: What signs, Symbols will remain?]

TASK 4. TO FIND AN ENDURING CONNECTION WITH THE DECEASED IN THE MIDST OF EMBARKING ON A NEW LIFE

[handwritten: Name losses?]

As I said previously, the purpose of our grief work is to relocate our lived experience of the person, place, or thing we have lost to an experience of memory. Psychiatrists Phyllis Silverman and Steven Nickman put it like this:

[handwritten: Recall other bldg changes]

> As mourners move on with their lives to find new roles, new directions, and new sources of gratification, they experience the past as very much a part of who they are. The deceased are both present and not present at the same time. It is possible to be bereft and not bereft simultaneously, to have a sense of continuity and yet to know that nothing will ever be the same.[15]

[handwritten: How carry forward?]

According to Worden, this final task involves learning how to live in the paradox Silverman and Nickman describe. Like the other tasks, our work finding a place for this lost relationship in our memories begins shortly after the loss occurs. Typically, at funerals and memorial services people tell stories about the person who has died in formal eulogies and informally at gatherings and meals associated with the service. This storytelling plays an important role in our grieving, and an opportunity is missed when community gatherings are skipped.

Frequently, at funerals and memorial services, only positive memories are shared, and more painful, negative aspects of the person's life are avoided. Over time, a more realistic picture of the deceased is often embraced by the bereaved as a broader range of stories are remembered and shared. Again, our cultural taboos around grieving often result in people avoiding the mention of the person who has died for fear of raising up painful memories and upsetting the bereaved person. This results in a conspiracy of silence growing up around the grieving person and makes the work of telling stories and creating realistic memories that much harder.

Similar storytelling takes place after other kinds of losses. After a disaster or other trauma neighbors, friends, and complete strangers gather to tell stories about what happened, supporting one another in their grief. Divorced partners recount the struggles that ended their marriage. I have told the story about losing my keys at a campground and having to hitchhike fifty miles to the closest dealership to get a replacement so many times, I think some of my friends could tell it themselves.

As time passes, our relationship with what was lost changes, and begins to function differently in the context of our lives. An "inner representation" of the deceased slowly replaces the external, physical relationship we once shared with the lost person, place, or thing. According to psychoanalyst W. D. Fairbairn, in the case of a significant death, this inner representation consists of those aspects of the self that are identified with the deceased, characteristics or thematic memories of the deceased, and the emotional states connected with those characterizations and memories.[16] In other words, the grieving person forms a picture of the deceased in their memory that is shaped by their lived experience with the person. For example, an adult son may see his deceased father in his own mannerisms, behaviors, and emotional reactions. A spouse may remember his wife's kindness and compassion and be moved to act more kindly or compassionately toward others. A friend may think about a companion's love of travel during a trip abroad and because of it, find greater appreciation in their own experience of a new place.

This inner representation manifests itself in the life of the grieving person in a number of ways. The deceased may be looked to as a role model, a source of guidance, or the clarifier of values and principles in the life of the bereaved person. Many grieving people report having an ongoing internal dialogue with the person who died as they make decisions, face challenges, engage others, and build new relationships. Characteristics of the deceased person can come to mind in times of joy and struggle: a laugh, a smile, a gentle spirit, an attitude of hard work or patient caring. Of course, the more negative aspects of the person who was lost can also influence us as we try to avoid the mistakes, bad habits, or difficult characteristics of the one who died. Initially, the inner dialogue with the deceased can hold a central place in the life of the grieving person. Over time, these bonds tend to play a less central and more infrequent role in the survivor's life. It is unlikely, though, that the memory will fade completely, as these inner representations of past relationships are deeply knit into the fabric of who we are.

As we build our continuing bonds to what we have lost in healthy ways, remembering, not forgetting, will provide us with a source of continuing strength and insight as we adapt to the loss and reengage life in new ways.

Check out rationale for initial bldg.

In Conversation

- As you think about your own experiences with loss and grief, which task has been the most challenging for you to work through?

  1. Accepting the reality of the loss
  2. Processing the pain of grief
  3. Adjusting to the world without the deceased (or what has been lost)
  4. Finding an enduring connection with the deceased (or what has been lost) while embarking on a new life

- Why? Who or what helped you overcome those challenges?
- How might your personal experiences and understanding of loss and grief shape or inform your response to loss and grief in your congregation?

BIBLE STUDY: 1 THESSALONIANS 4:13–14

Paul's warm letter to the Thessalonian church is considered the earliest letter we have from the apostle. The community at Thessalonica is asking questions about the coming of the Lord and raising concerns about those who have died.

1. Read 1 Thessalonians 4:13–14.

2. Reflect on and then discuss the following questions:

- How can hope change the way we think about and work through the tasks of grieving discussed in this chapter? As individuals? As a congregation?

- How can our hope in the future resurrection influence the way we live in the here and now? How might it inform how we think about the past?

- In concrete terms, how might our hope in Christ help us to face whatever challenges confront us in the future?

A Cloud of Witnesses: Nostalgia, Yearning, and the Past

Therefore, since we are surrounded by so great a cloud of witnesses, let us also lay aside every weight and the sin that clings so closely, and let us run with perseverance the race that is set before us. (Heb 12:1)

Three old farmers sat on the front porch looking out over the sea of corn and soybeans that stretched to the South Dakota horizon. The crops were just starting to turn from green to golden. "I remember when there was a family living on just about every section," the first farmer mused, rocking slowly back in his chair, a sentimental glint in his eye.

"I remember riding with my dad on his old tractor. Open to the weather. Sun. Wind. Li'l rain. Didn't matter. He was out there working," the second reminisced wistfully, his gravelly voice carrying a fondness for simpler times.

"I remember a lot of dust," the third said bluntly.

As we remember the past and grieve the empty places in

our lives once filled by people, places, and things now lost to us, we can either get trapped in those memories as we yearn for that which is gone, or we can use those memories to build the continuing bonds that can carry us into the future. Nostalgia and yearning are often thought to be synonymous terms for remembering the past, but increasingly we are learning that they are not. Just as we are learning that grief is not about relinquishing emotional attachments to that which we've lost, we are also learning that nostalgia can actually contribute to building the continuing bonds and inner representations that we carry with us into the future. While yearning ties us to the past and can lead to our becoming stuck in our grief, nostalgia can open us to the great cloud of witnesses the writer of Hebrews describes and help us to draw from their example as we contemplate our future.

The New Oxford American Dictionary defines "nostalgia" as "a sentimental longing or wistful affection for the past, typically for a period or place with happy personal associations."

In Conversation

Think about an experience that makes you nostalgic. Take a few minutes and write out the story.

It is common for people to engage in nostalgia. According to sociologist and nostalgia researcher Clay Routledge, in one study, 74 percent of eighteen-to-thirty-year-olds reported experiencing nostalgia at least once a week, and only 15 percent reported that they are nostalgic less than monthly.[1] Similar experiences are reported across all ages. Reflecting longingly and wistfully on the past is a human characteristic and always has been. We find examples of nostalgia going back as long as people have been telling stories about who they are and where they come from.

36

Often nostalgia is related to meaningful or momentous events from our past. Frequently they are associated with pleasant experiences and happy memories.

In Conversation

When you think about an experience that makes you feel nostalgic, what came to mind? Share your story with your group.

- Who was part of the nostalgic memory that came to you?
- Who was with you?
- What other people were around?

Nostalgic memories usually involve others. Nostalgic memories can include close relationships, childhood friends, family members, or colleagues being there for or with us at key points in our lives. Through nostalgic reflection we can reconnect with important others who were meaningful to us and to our lives.

In Conversation

Read back over your nostalgic memory.

- What role did you play in your story?
- What did you do or say?
- How did you act?
- Were you at center stage, in the cast, or off stage in the wings?

While nostalgic memories are often peopled by significant others, we are almost always at the center of these personal stories. As a friend of mine puts it, we are usually the heroes (or, I suppose, antiheroes) of our own novels. Nostalgia is always a memory told from our perspective, seen through our eyes, and edited through our own filters. Others who were a part of the experience will almost certainly have a different story to tell. I know. My mother and I often have very different memories about things that happened in my childhood. And, of course, my telling is always right! In truth, so is hers.

This filtered quality of nostalgic memory can be seen in the wilderness stories following Israel's exodus from Egypt. After leaving Egypt, the Israelites find themselves getting nostalgic about their days in the Nile delta. The book of Numbers reports it like this:

> The rabble among them had a strong craving; and the Israelites also wept again, and said, "If only we had meat to eat! We remember the fish we used to eat in Egypt for nothing, the cucumbers, the melons, the leeks, the onions, and the garlic; but now our strength is dried up, and there is nothing at all but this manna to look at." (Num 11:4–6)

It is striking that the Israelites managed to remember all the good things about their sojourn in the land of Egypt but somehow managed to forget all about the abuses of their taskmasters, making bricks in the hot sun, the killing of their firstborns at Pharaoh's decree, and all the other terrible things they had endured.

Nostalgia can be like that. Our memories can be notoriously faulty, especially when we are remembering favorite experiences and pleasant times. We recall the good, the positive, and the happy memories of times past, scrubbed of the challenges, hardships, and struggles that surrounded them. That is one of the reasons the happy personal associations of nostalgic remembering can generate feelings of loss and the experience of grief. The remembered past can draw forth feelings of sadness and loneliness as we think about people who are no longer with us and experiences that will never be repeated. Nostalgia is often bittersweet.

NOSTALGIA AND GRIEF

Because of the bittersweet nature of nostalgia and its ability to conjure up feelings of grief, nostalgia was long thought to be an unhealthy and problematic human behavior. Though the wistful reverie we call nostalgia has been around as long as there have been people who remember the past, the term itself was coined in 1688 by Swiss medical student Johannes Hofer.[2] He created the term from two Greek words, *nostos* (to return home) and *algos* (pain), to describe the yearning for home he observed in soldiers fighting in distant battlefields. Nostalgia was viewed as a neurological or medical illness well into the nineteenth century. According to researchers Constantine Sedikides and Tim Wildschut of the Center for Research on Self and Identity at the University of Southampton, by the mid-twentieth century, nostalgia was considered a "regressive manifestation closely related to the issue of loss, grief, incomplete mourning, and, finally, depression."[3]

In contrast to these traditional understandings of nostalgia, the research of Routledge, Sedikides, Wildschut, and others has demonstrated that nostalgia is a human coping mechanism that helps us adapt to the present by drawing strength from past experiences. Nostalgia may refer to the past, but, unlike yearning, it tends to be forward-looking. Nostalgic thinking provides a sense of continuity with the past, linking the past to the present, and opening up possibilities for the future. Unlike yearning, which traps us in the past, nostalgia is a dynamic and motivational force that can help us take proactive action as we step into the future.[4] Nostalgia and nostalgic memories can help convince us that if we accomplished something once, we can accomplish something similar again. If we felt loved, cared for, and supported in the past, nostalgia can make us hopeful that we can experience those feelings again. Though the past cannot be re-created, nostalgic memory is a tool for drawing insights, wisdom, knowledge, and skill from previous experiences.

NOSTALGIA AND BELONGING

By connecting us to past experiences and the people who were a significant part of those experiences, nostalgia reinforces our sense of belonging. All of us have a need to belong.[5] From the very beginning, we were created to be together. In Genesis 2:18 God says, "It is not good that the man should be alone; I will make him a helper as his partner." Throughout the Scriptures, God is always calling people into community. Jesus started his ministry by building a community. He called the Twelve to walk with him, learn from him, and continue his mission after the resurrection.

After a significant death, grief causes us to disengage from our social worlds for a time as we reorient ourselves to life without the deceased. Routledge's survey of research into nostalgia shows that nostalgia can bolster our social functioning. This research suggests that nostalgic memories can be useful tools in breaking down the inward-focused isolation that is a natural part of the grief process and can move us toward reconnecting with our social world in new ways.

Because nostalgic memories tend to be social in nature, they can increase our feelings of social connectedness. Nostalgia can strengthen social bonds, assure us that those around us can and will support and care for us, engender trust, and lower intergroup anxiety. Nostalgic memories can affirm our sense of social confidence and inspire us to risk reaching out to others and form new relationships with them. Nostalgia has been shown to influence social engagement by increasing empathy, charity, and helpfulness.

Nostalgia also increases self-image, self-esteem, and sense of self-efficacy, all of which can be battered by the experience of loss. Nostalgia can help us imagine the person we want to become by reminding us of the person we used to be. Nostalgic memories connect us to role models from our past who have formed us along the way, including those we have lost by death or whom we have lost touch with over the years.

In a world that is constantly changing, nostalgic memories can foster a connection between one's past and present self, building up a sense of self-continuity that is an important human need.[6] Maintaining a sense of self-continuity is especially important when we have experienced the potentially shattering feelings of separation and deprivation caused by significant losses. This need to preserve self-continuity is a further argument for building continuing bonds with the past rather than dissecting those attachments and letting go of our memories of the people and things we have lost. *Harald*

Nostalgic memories make us more mindful of who we are in the present. Staying connected to our past strengthens our self-identity, which can give us the courage and the wisdom to step into what appears to be an uncertain future.

Recently, I had a long conversation with a dear friend and colleague whom I've known for years. We visit quite regularly in brief phone calls, emails, and texts. But on this occasion we had the luxury of time. It wasn't long into our visit that we started to reminisce about the adventures and misadventures we have shared together. We remembered people and places long since gone. There was loss and grief and gratitude wrapped around those memories. Nostalgia filled the space between us like the warmth of a fireplace on a cold afternoon. As we reminisced, the past and the present spoke to one another as the conversation drifted in and out of the present realities and challenges in our lives.

When we were finished, I felt better, and so did my friend. We agreed that we needed to have conversations like that more often. The continuing bonds between us and our mutual memories strengthened us for whatever lay ahead.

In Conversation

- What are some of the key stories from your past that inform your life in the present?
- What have you learned from them?
- What else might you learn?
- How do they shape you as a person and the way you interact with others?

CONGREGATIONS AND NOSTALGIA

As congregations think about their past, calling up nostalgic memories can free us from the trap of yearning for how things used to be and help us reconnect with the energy, creativity, and inspiration of the "glory days" in the life of the parish. Like the people of Israel who nostalgically looked back on their time in the wilderness as the time when they were closest to God, our own nostalgic reflection can help us see how the Holy Spirit was at work among us, the gospel of Jesus Christ was motivating us, and the God who created us and called us was with us in those days. That reflection can give us assurance that God is still with us, even as we acknowledge and grieve what we have lost, and give us the courage and strength to trust that God will lead us through our own wilderness times.

PROLONGED GRIEF

As we work through the tasks of grief, it is possible for us to get "stuck" along the journey. This sense of being stuck in one's grief has been referred to by a variety of names: abnormal grief, pathological grief, unresolved grief, prolonged grief, and complicated grief. Because the grief process is so unique to each loss and to each individual, it is sometimes difficult to determine when a normal grief process has become "stuck" or abnormal. The context of the loss, the nature of the relationship with what has been lost, the circumstances leading up to the loss, and the personal characteristics and health of the griever can make the grief process more difficult. In most cases, rather than trying to determine whether a person's grief process is normal or abnormal, it is more helpful to simply acknowledge the complexity of some grief processes and the likelihood that the person will need help negotiating those complexities. When someone comes to me and expresses their concerns that they feel stuck in their grief, I take that seriously and, depending on the issues, help them find a counselor or therapist to work with them in getting unstuck. For example, Carol, whom we met at the beginning of part 1, took a long time to bring herself to even dust her child's room after her child died. I referred her to a counselor, because I was afraid her grief was becoming unhealthy. As it turned out, while her grief was complex and her grief process slow, and there were many "stuck" moments along the way, in her case it was completely normal, given the circumstances surrounding her loss.

In some cases, however, it is clear that an individual's grief has become stuck to the point of being unhealthy. Criteria for determining what is and what is not unhealthy grief have been developed by individual researchers, the American Psychiatric Association (APA), and other groups over the years. For the first time, the eleventh revision of the World Health Organization's International Classification of Diseases (ICD) includes diagnostic criteria for "prolonged grief disorder." According to the ICD,

> Prolonged grief disorder is a disturbance in which, following the death of a partner, parent, child, or other person close to the bereaved, there is persistent and pervasive grief response characterized by longing for the deceased or persistent preoc-

43

cupation with the deceased accompanied by intense emotional pain.[7]

The key to diagnosis is the enduring, long-term, and disruptive nature of the symptoms. Symptoms of intense emotional pain, including sadness, yearning, anger, blame, numbness, and social disengagement are experienced during normal grieving but tend to resolve themselves over time. In prolonged grief disorder, symptoms that would be considered normal in the early days following a loss continue unabated. Instead of seeing the gradual dissipation of intense and debilitating grief, a mourner continues to experience this level of grief almost daily for months or even years.

The APA diagnostic criteria for "persistent complex bereavement-related disorder" offers a list of symptoms similar to those named in the ICD definition, but where the ICD requires clinically significant symptoms to be present for at least six months, the APA requires at least six symptoms to be present on most days to a clinically significant degree for at least twelve months after the death in order for it to be considered persistent complex bereavement.[8] Other than her inability to face her son's room, Carol was working through many other aspects of her grief. She needed help to overcome her fear of forgetting her child but was coping well with many other parts of her life. While Carol's grief didn't fit the diagnostic criteria for prolonged grief disorder, the complicated nature of her loss called for some additional guidance and support.

Though both the APA and ICD definitions of prolonged grief disorder are, in part, determined by the persistence of the symptoms of intense grief over time, in American popular culture, bereaved individuals often expect the symptoms of grief to resolve themselves quickly. Frequently, people working through their grief will ask, "How long will this last?"

They are often concerned about whether their grief has become abnormal or unhealthy, because their grief responses have persisted longer than expected. Even after a highly significant loss, individuals expect to be back to normal in a month or two. My response to this concern for a timeline is generally, "As long as it takes . . . as long as you keep working through what you are thinking and feeling." I am much more focused on the effect the grief is having and whether the person is continuing to work through the emotions and other reactions associated with the grief.

Intense yearning, one of the symptoms of prolonged grief disorder, is a common barrier that prevents people from adapting to the changed reality and embracing new opportunities in life. In the early part of a grief process reminiscing is natural and even plays a necessary role in creating an inner representation of the person who died. However, if the fixation on the past persists, it can become problematic and needs to be investigated further with a counselor or therapist. Persistent yearning can leave us stuck in our grief, unable to move forward out of fear we will lose our connection with whatever we have lost. In the case of a death, out of fear we will forget our deceased loved one.

"Living in the past" contributes to ongoing social disengagement and an inability to form new relationships, or adapt to changed circumstances. Psychologists Alexander Jordan and Brett Litz, in their article on prolonged grief disorder, describe the effect of complicated grief on the bereaved: "Disengaged from the social sphere, the bereaved may thus keep his or her attention narrowly fixed on the past and the meaning, pleasure, and intimacy it contained before the loss of the loved one."[9]

Ramona rarely went out. She spent most of her days sitting in her recliner inside her small, dilapidated home. The old house was the last one left from a neighborhood that had

45

been slowly giving way to strip malls, office buildings, and gas stations. Every month or six weeks, I would stop by to bring Ramona Communion, read Scripture with her, pray, and reminisce. For the most part, Ramona lived in the past. When she told me about days gone by, her usually sad eyes would light up, and her face would come alive. She would tell me the same stories about her husband and son over and over as if the events she narrated had happened recently. I knew better. Her husband had been gone for well over ten years. Her son had died suddenly shortly after her husband. Ramona's daughter had explained that to me early in my ministry in that place. "She's been living in the past ever since my brother died," though by the time I arrived, some dementia had begun to set in as well.

It was clear to me that Ramona's grief had trapped her in the past. Nothing inside her house had changed since her son's death. No one had ever addressed her grief or considered that it might be the cause of her continual reminiscing. She had never seen a counselor or therapist, though she and her daughter had spoken with her family doctor about it a few times. Ramona seemed content living in a world that was long gone. Her family just accepted the fact that this was the way she was and weren't interested in pursuing it further.

In Conversation

- Have you ever felt "stuck" in your grief?
- What helped you get unstuck?
- If you feel stuck right now, what steps might you take to address your unresolved grief?
- Who might you turn to?

CONGREGATIONS AND COMPLICATED GRIEF

Like Ramona, congregations can get stuck in their past, reminiscing about days gone by, telling nostalgic stories about the good times, sharing memories about busy Sunday schools, crowded pews, and dynamic activities and events. In telling those stories there is always a bittersweet mix of happy memories and sadness that things aren't like that anymore. The grief in the telling of these stories is often palpable.

Jordan and Litz's description of the effect of prolonged grief disorder can be seen in declining congregations yearning for their lost past. These congregations often disengage from the community around them and stop participating in denominational activities and events. Yearning for the lost meaning, pleasure, and intimacy of the past leaves congregations unwilling to consider any change that doesn't promise a return to the "glory days."

As we now turn our attention to consider the grief process in congregational life, we will explore what it means to reimagine our relationship with the past. Rather than letting go of the past or getting stuck there, we will ask what it means to remember our past in healthy ways, even as we acknowledge that we cannot re-create the past and need to grieve what we perceive we have lost. Once we have worked through our grief at the loss of the past, our continuing bonds with our own story can both strengthen our ministries and provide us with the wisdom to make decisions, face challenges, engage others, and build new relationships as we embark on the future to which God is calling us. As we will discover, nostalgia and nostalgic memories can help us move beyond yearning and tap into these inner representations to draw out the strength and wisdom they offer.

BIBLE STUDY: HEBREWS 12:1–2

In Hebrews 11, the writer reminds the readers of some of the great examples of faithfulness in the history of God's people. In Hebrews 12:1–2, the writer invites the readers to consider the past, and especially the story of Jesus, to find encouragement and hope for the present and future. This text encourages readers to think nostalgically about these heroes of the faith.

1. Read Hebrews 12:1–2.

2. Explore how this passage applies to your own experience.

    *   On a piece of paper, write the name of three people who are a part of your "cloud of witnesses" and a sentence or two describing how they demonstrated faithfulness.

    *   Pick one of these witnesses and share their story with your group. In larger groups you may want to divide into pairs for this sharing.

    *   What do these stories have in common? What sets them apart?

    *   What might you learn from them about facing loss and grief in your life? In the life of your congregation?

3. The writer of Hebrews points to Jesus as the "pioneer and perfecter of our faith" (v. 2). He endured the cross so that we might not grow weary or lose heart. Remembering Jesus is the church's ultimate nostalgic memory.

- How might the presence of Jesus help us face what we have lost and work through the grief we experience?

- How can the memory of Jesus's life, death, and resurrection sustain us as we consider the future?

PART II

Litany of Lament: The Reality of Loss in Congregational Life

God is our refuge and strength,

a very present help in trouble. (Ps 46:1)

"Come with me!" I urged my friend. We were standing in the long hall of a hotel conference center outside a row of meeting rooms. I was trying to convince him to join me for a workshop called "The Future of the Church." I knew the presenter and was hoping to pick up some new perspectives and ideas about where the church was going and how to help the faith community I was serving get there.

"I was going to take a nap," my friend grumbled and then reluctantly followed me into the meeting room.

The lecture, illustrated with charts and graphs, started with a lengthy presentation on the "life cycle of a church." The presenter talked about the heady, exciting days of a new mission start. He explained that as those nascent congregations grew and launched new programs and ministries, they had energy and enthusiasm to take risks and do things like set up and take down folding chairs in a school gym each week. He moved on to talk about the plateau years, when the traditions and patterns of programs, worship, roles, and relationships became established and a status quo emerged. Finally, he talked about years of decline and, finally, the death of the congregation.

He suggested that the only way to circumvent this cycle of birth, maturity, and decline was to intervene and help the congregation be creative and innovative during the height of the cycle, when everything was going well. Waiting to intervene until the congregation moved into decline made it difficult, if not impossible, to turn things around.

That scenario was bleak enough, especially when I thought about many of the congregations I knew that were definitely on the downhill slope of his graphs. It was depressing to think many of them were hopeless causes.

But then, he moved on to talk about the state of mainline denominations. It was clear that, in his opinion, they were over the peak and headed precipitously down the slope of decline. He warned that if we didn't do something soon, the deaths of these denominations were soon to follow.

That was it. That was where the workshop ended. No word of hope. No word of encouragement. No suggestions for how to "do something soon" to address the bleak picture he painted.

My friend and I walked out of the workshop dejected, a gloomy cloud hanging over us. "Don't ever invite me to another workshop," my friend said as we walked slowly down the long hall of the conference center. I couldn't blame him. I knew how he felt. We both carried a rock of helplessness and hopelessness . . . of grief . . . in the pits of our stomachs.

I swore to myself that I would never, ever leave a group or congregation hanging hopeless like that. I pray I have been true to that promise.

Even before attending this workshop, I had thought that recounting tales of decline was unhelpful to congregations. The workshop only confirmed that belief. What good was it to dwell on the bleak path that inevitably led to death? How helpful was it to climb into the pit of ashes and just sit there? Though I was certainly willing to respond to a congregation's litany of lament—a recounting of its experience of change, decline, and loss—when leaders and members brought it up, I preferred to move on quickly to talk about ways to address the changes they had experienced.

Since then, I have learned from observation and hard experience that until we come to terms with our laments about the lost past, it is hard to even begin thinking more creatively about the opportunities of the future. The sense of loss, and the helplessness and hopelessness that come with it, can become an insurmountable barrier to turning things around and embracing God's future. Denying, avoiding, or attempting to circumvent the grief that comes from these laments can put a congregation on the inevitable path to death that the presenter described at his workshop.

The way to deal with the litany of lament the presenter and many congregations sing is not to pretend there is nothing to lament or attempt to skip over the lament and get on with the problem-solving. We also cannot deal with it by curling up in a ball on the couch to wait for the end to come. Instead, we need to recognize the reality of the loss and its impact on our congregations, acknowledge the grief, and, with the courage of our faith, work through it—as hard as that can be. After all, as people of faith, we do not grieve as those with no hope.

Telling Your Congregation's Story of Life and Loss

So far, we have looked at the experience of loss and how losses affect our individual lives, learned some of the basic principles behind a task-based model of grief, and introduced an understanding of nostalgia that suggests it is a resource for drawing strength from our past for the sake of embracing the future. Now, as we turn to thinking about your own congregation's experience with loss and reflecting on the litany of lament your particular community of faith sings, I would like you to take some significant time to lay out the story of your congregation in some detail by developing a timeline that reflects your congregation's experiences in mission and ministry. We'll be adding to this timeline and reflecting on it throughout the rest of the book as we learn how we might embrace God's future without forgetting the past. If your congregation has a written history, you might want to read through it before starting this exercise.

When working with grieving people, storytelling is one of the most important ways people get in touch with their experience of loss, the emotions and other reactions of grief, and the meaning of the loss for their lives. Storytelling facilitates healing and hope and opens one up to the possibilities for the future.

When I was teaching my "Death: Grief and Growth" class in the university, I was often asked what the class was about. Kidding, I would reply, "It's a how-to course." Actually, I wasn't kidding. The class was about learning how the reality of death shapes our lives as human beings. On the first day of class I would always say, "This is not a class about death. It is a class about living life with the death left in it." The timeline you will be creating in this exercise and in the "In Conversation" discussion that follows will help you tell your congregation's story with the loss left in it.

You'll need to start by getting a roll of newsprint. These can be found at moving or packing stores, or as "end rolls" at newspaper offices that still print their own paper. If you can't find a roll of newsprint, use sheets of newsprint paper. If you use newsprint sheets, I would suggest using one sheet for each decade of the congregation's life. It will be helpful to have several sets of colored markers available for this exercise.

Start by unrolling several feet of the newsprint on tables set end to end (two or three, depending on how old your congregation is). It will be easier if you do this in a larger room with space to spread out. On this newsprint you will be laying out the basic timeline of your congregation from its founding to the present day. Draw a horizontal line one-quarter of the way from the top edge of the paper and mark off the decades.

Now, arrange your group members according to how long you've been a member or participant in the life of the congregation. When facing the paper, the long-term members should be to the left, the relative newcomers to the right. This way, those who have been around the longest can chart the earliest days of the congregation, and the newcomers can work on the part of the timeline when they have been involved.

Next, each person should mark on the timeline the year when they joined the congregation. After noting this, spend a few minutes talking about what brought you to join this community of faith. Who played a role in your joining? What memories about this congregation make you feel nostalgic?

After everyone has had a chance to tell their personal story, lay out as much of the congregation's story as you can. If you have a congregation historian or archive committee, you might invite that person or group to be a part of this exercise. If there are still charter members around, you might want to invite them too. You can either do this work in smaller groups, with each group taking a decade, or all together, depending on the size of your group. Note significant events, the coming and going of pastors or other significant leaders, important anniversaries, the beginning and ending of programs, building projects, and other key projects. If there are gaps in the timeline, you may need to do some homework to finish it.

Here are some questions you should consider:

- When was the congregation founded? Who was the founding pastor? What key events led up to and immediately followed the congregation's founding?

- Who were the pastors who served the congregation and what years did they serve?

- Were there years when you had an interim or vice pastor? No pastor at all? Make sure to mark down those transition years and significant events and activities during those years.

57

staff

- Are there other leaders who should be noted? For example, an organist, music director, youth director, secretaries or administrators, volunteers, and so on.

- How many places have housed your congregation over the years? Where did you worship when the ministry first began? When were buildings built? Added on to or remodeled? Destroyed or damaged by fire or flood or wind or some other disaster?

- What key programs, ministries, activities, celebrations, or other events do you remember?

Draw a second line in the middle of the page. Now, go back through the timeline and, using a different-color marker or pen, identify the losses your congregation has experienced.

- When did the pastors who served you leave? What were the circumstances of their departure?

During one of these conversations in a congregation I thought I knew well, I learned about a pastor who left on vacation and died in a fiery car accident along with his whole family. No one ever talked about it, and yet, when I heard the story, lightbulbs came on. I suddenly understood some puzzling behaviors I had observed in the congregation like their habit of keeping their pastors at arm's length, their resistance to the pastor taking time off, and their excessive concern about all the driving I do as their bishop.

- When were there conflicts? Divisions? Disagreements? When did they begin? How and when were they resolved (if ever)?

- If you changed buildings, what losses were experienced as the congregation moved from one place to another?

- What significant departures and deaths do you remember? The last charter member? A key leader moving away? The tragic death of a child?

I know of one medium-sized congregation (about 150 in worship) that lost ten key members to death in one year! Those deaths resulted in the loss of a number of leaders, longtime friends, and around 20 percent of the congregation's annual budget. The grief from those losses convinced the congregation they no longer had the resources to do ministry, paralyzed their ability to think creatively about the future, and had them contemplating closing . . . though, in reality, they still had more than enough people and resources to continue in ministry.

- What other losses has the congregation experienced? Remember to think about symbolic as well as tangible losses.

Draw a third line three-quarters of the way from the top of the paper. As best as you can, mark down any significant events in your local community, state, province or region, and nation. Again, you might need to do a little research before completing this third line. Note how significant events in the world around you affected your congregation.

In Conversation

After you have finished your work, talk about what you see.

- Do events on the three lines align in any significant way?
- Do your experiences of loss connect with changes in the congregation or in the world around you?
- What patterns begin to emerge?
- What cycles repeat themselves?
- If your congregation is in decline, when did that downward trend start?
- What was going on both inside and outside your congregation when that happened?
- If you are growing, consider the same questions.

4

The Story of Loss: Ministry in a World of Change

But God chose what is foolish in the world to shame the wise;
God chose what is weak in the world to shame the strong. (1
Cor 1:27)

Accepting the reality of the losses we face is the first task
of grieving.[1] In the task-based approach to mourning we
have been exploring, "acceptance" means acknowledging the
losses we have experienced, understanding how those losses
affect us and actively working through the resulting grief.
Congregations, like individuals whose loved ones have died,
are usually quite capable of naming the changes they have
witnessed and the losses that have accompanied them. The
litany of lament is all too common. We have been singing it
for years. We all know the words.

Aging members
Empty pews
Lack of young families, children, and youth

Declining offerings

The inability to afford a pastor

Deteriorating buildings

Lack of participation

The end of long-standing programs, ministries, and events

You might add a few losses of your own to the list.

But simply recognizing the losses we have experienced is just the beginning of the process of accepting the reality of those losses.[2] Loss is rarely the result of straight-line cause and effect. Instead, loss and the grief that follows result from a complex interplay of both external and internal factors. Events and interactions both within the congregation and in the outside world mutually influence one another and result in patterns of behavior that become repeated within the life of the congregation.[3] Changes in the world both inside and outside the congregation frequently lead to losses, which, as they pile up, compound one another and lead to the litanies of lament we so often sing. If a congregation does not come to terms with the changes it has experienced and acknowledge the losses that have resulted from those changes, it will likely remain stuck in the grief from those losses and be unable to work on the other tasks of the grief process.

THE WORLD AROUND US

Take another look at the third line on your timeline. If your congregation is like most, events in the world around you have had an impact on both the growth and decline of your congregation. A suburban community experiences a period of rapid growth, and the congregation swells. An urban community experiences a time of "white flight," and the membership dwindles away or begins commuting from the suburbs. A natural disaster triggers a period of struggle and financial challenge as members rebuild their lives. The losses and gains resulting from these local events can be easy to see. But our

62

congregations have also been affected by macro changes in the world around us that may be more difficult to discern. Some of the losses related to these changes have come on us at glacial speed and so have been hard to recognize and accept. However, these very losses are often the ones that draw forth the main verses of our litany of lament.

We cannot deny that the social and cultural world around our congregations has changed dramatically in the last seventy years or so. These changes have resulted in change and loss for the church as well. Because we live in unsettled times, the traditional ways of doing ministry many of us grew up with no longer seem to work. As a pastor, I was trained primarily to care for the gathered congregation: to lead worship, preach, teach Bible studies, provide pastoral care, welcome new members, and preside at weddings, funerals, and other life events. Evangelism, community engagement, and outreach were minor parts of my education. If it hadn't been for my years in campus ministry and some very fine mentors, I would have no idea how to grow a community of faith, renew one in decline, or start a new ministry from scratch.

As we consider the litany of lament sung by many congregations and the losses reflected in that lament, it is important for us to realize that the church is not the only social institution in North America to be unsettled by the changes that have occurred since the middle of the last century or to experience the decline and loss that have resulted. The decline in the church is part of a larger pattern of erosion in social participation and civic engagement that has taken place in the United States since the mid-1960s.

In 2000, political scientist Robert Putnam released his extensive demographic analysis and review of social participation, civic engagement, and social connectedness in the United States since the end of World War II called *Bowling Alone*. While *Bowling Alone* is a serious academic study,

Putnam's book made its way to popular book lists because so many could identify with his portrayal of change in American society. In the book, Putnam traces the decline in participation in a broad array of social organizations, including card clubs, dinner parties, community and civic organizations, unions, bowling leagues, community meetings, and churches. He identifies declines in community-focused activities like voting, volunteering, altruism, and philanthropy, and in community-centered values like reciprocity, honesty, and trust.[4]

 According to Putnam's research, social participation in the United States, in all its many forms, increased substantially between 1947 and 1965 and then significantly decreased between 1965 and 1998.[5] It is no coincidence that many new congregations were established and older congregations expanded during the years social participation was expanding and that many of those same congregations are now struggling with declining membership and the attendant losses.

In his study, Putnam identifies and examines a number of factors that have contributed to the decline in civic engagement and social capital in the United States since 1965. Such a broad change in behaviors, he argues, can be attributed not to a single cause (as we so often try to do), but to a variety of factors working together to bring about the observed changes.[6] Putnam's list includes the rise in two-career families, suburbanization, the effect of electronic entertainment and especially television (and in the decades since his study, the rise of social media), and, according to Putnam, most important, generational change. Putnam argues that the high level of civic involvement and social participation of the "greatest generation" that came of age during and immediately following World War II was simply not replicated in their baby-boom children and Gen-X grandchildren. Time will tell whether the current generation of young adults and the children and youth following them will be more or less involved in social life than those who came before them. There is evidence that the millennial generation (born 1981–1996) will be more socially involved than their baby-boom parents, but their involvement does not tend to be expressed through large organizations and institutions like churches. This is very different from their grandparents' and great-grandparents' way of social participation.

In Conversation

Putnam identifies a number of social organizations other than the church that have experienced decline.

- Have other social groups or organizations in your community experienced these changes too?
- How has the decline in community-focused activities he identifies affected your congregation?

Review the losses you listed on your timeline.

- How might changes in patterns of social participation have contributed to any of these losses?

THE "GOLDEN AGE"

Statistically, what many older members remember as the "golden age" of church growth and activity in the postwar years was part of the broader boom in social participation and civic engagement evidenced across mainstream American culture during those years. In reality, those years were the "anomaly" that has become the nostalgic norm for thriving church life many of us hold in our memories.

My own denomination, the Evangelical Lutheran Church in America (ELCA), provides a good example of these broader trends. In 1940, the baptized membership of the predecessor bodies to the ELCA (which was formed in 1988)

65

totaled 3,117,626. During the period from 1947 to 1965, the years Putnam identifies as the period of dramatic growth in social participation, the membership of the ELCA's predecessor bodies ballooned to a peak of 5,887,093. That is a growth of over 2 million members in less than fifteen years![7] Since reaching the peak in membership in 1965, the membership of the ELCA has slowly declined to 3,563,842, almost back to its 1940 numbers.[8]

These numbers reflect the nationwide trends in social participation identified by Putnam. They also reflect a decline in religious participation across US Christian denominations and other faith traditions identified in ongoing studies by both Gallup and Pew Research. For example, in 2016, Pew Research reported that only 36 percent of adults say they worship weekly, while 30 percent say they worship seldom or never. The weekly-worship participation rate is down from almost 50 percent in the mid-1950s.[9] Membership in faith communities has dropped from a high of 76 percent of Americans in the late 1940s to around 56 percent in 2016. Those who say that religion is important in their lives have dropped from 70 percent in 1968 to 53 percent in 2016.[10]

In Conversation

On your timeline, chart the membership and worship attendance in your congregation as far back as possible.

- Do your numbers reflect the broader trends Putnam and polls describe?
- If so, what do you think this means?
- If not, why not?
- If your congregation was established after 1965, how do your participation and membership trends reflect what was happening in your community? Think about significant events—community experiences like tragedies, storms, or disasters; economic changes like new employers coming or businesses closing; and population growth or decline.

CHANGES IN PATTERNS OF BELONGING

It has been twenty years since Putnam published his study, and the trends he notes have only deepened. But as Putnam traces the pattern of declining social participation, he also notes the growth in "personal communities" or "communities of limited liability." Putnam writes,

> Large groups with local chapters, long histories, multiple objectives, and diverse constituencies are being replaced by more evanescent, single-purpose organizations, smaller groups that "reflect the fluidity of our lives by allowing us to bond easily but to break our attachments with equivalent ease."[11]

Denominations, being "large groups with local chapters" and so forth, have witnessed these shifts in their pews and programs. For example, single-focus groups have become more prevalent. Small-group ministry has flourished in many places. Individuals seek out religious groups that meet their needs, often crossing denominational lines and participating in more than one religious community at a time. Spiritually focused groups with specific emphases like meditation, yoga, or social-justice ministry have become popular on social media.

People "belong" not only to small groups but also to large organizations like the AARP, NPR, or the NRA, although the meaning of that belonging has changed dramatically. Physical participation in these organizations is neither emphasized nor expected. Putnam argues that "place-based" social capital is being supplanted by "function-based" social capital.[12] In other words, as a culture, our commitments are more to organizations, activities, and programs that fulfill a specific need or function, rather than to a particular place or community of belonging like a congregation with a building and a fixed address. Participation in these function-based groups is often limited in duration as members' needs and interests change.

Even for those who are still members of a church, "belonging" no longer means what it once did—showing up weekly for worship. As of 2015, 57.9 percent of US congregations had fewer than one hundred people at weekend worship services. This was the first time since the early twentieth century that the number of congregations with average worship attendance under one hundred has exceeded 50 percent.[13] For many people in our culture, regular worship attendance is no longer a priority. In urban and suburban communities, people no longer live or work in the communities where they worship. Shaped by the consumerist culture of choice that emerged with the advent of the baby-boom generation, many people engage religious institutions not seeking communities of support and meaning but "shopping" for religious services. This consumerist understanding of "membership" can be observed when people come to the church for functional reasons like baptisms, weddings, funerals, or other services. Like people who belong to the AARP, NPR, and the NRA, people consider themselves members but do not expect to meet face-to-face with other members. Consistent with the function-based understanding of social organizations, they rarely attend because they don't feel like they need the services the church offers.

In one church I served, we did an evaluation of the membership rolls and reached out to people whom we had not recently seen, in some cases for many years. We were surprised how many of them still considered themselves to be members in good standing. In other cases, parents expressed a desire to maintain their children on church membership rolls, even though the children were living in distant communities with no intention of returning to the communities where they grew up.

While the decline in church participation parallels the general change in social participation and civic engagement in the United States as measured by Putnam, Gallup News, Pew Research, and others, evidence also suggests the decline in participation is not due to a loss of faith. Gallup reports that 89 percent of Americans still claim to believe in God or a universal spirit.[14] People still believe. It's just that they are expressing that belief differently. In my experience, for many people this means that faith in God has become a subtext in their lives rather than a central, integrating relationship that defines who they are and how they live. — Not sure that was true a.

Understanding these trends can help us more clearly understand the losses we have experienced in our congregations. Our failure to recognize these external changes and adapt our way of doing ministry to the realities they present has often led to loss and change within the life of our congregations. These internal changes often lead to secondary losses that resulted in further change. For us to work through the grief these losses bring, it is critical that we recognize the losses and understand them and the impact they have on our congregational systems.

RECOGNIZING THE LOSS

Accepting the reality of the losses we have experienced requires more than simply naming them. Working through this first task of the grief process also means recognizing the impact the loss has had on our lives.[15] A significant loss shatters an individual's sense of balance by disrupting the meaning, orderliness, and predictability of their life. In the same way, the stability of a congregation can be disrupted by loss. When this happens the congregation's system of relationships and interactions can become imbalanced, resulting in efforts to restore the equilibrium.[16] Acknowledging and understanding the facts of the loss begins the process of restoring that sense of balance as the congregation internalizes those facts. In the previous section, we considered some of the changing external realities that underlie the change and loss many congregations have experienced. But until we begin to understand the impact of those losses on the congregation's life together, we cannot fully accept the reality of those losses or the implications those losses have for the congregation's self-concept and their practice of ministry.

I saw this phenomenon in a very real way the first time I met with the people of St. James Church. Fifteen of us were sitting together in a circle in the center of the congregation's cavernous gymnasium talking about the future of their church. They were pretty much all that was left of a once large and thriving congregation. The youngest in the circle was just past retirement age; the eldest, over ninety. As they went around the circle, I asked them to share their names, how long they had been members, and something about the congregation and its ministry. It was striking that no one talked about their current ministry. Instead, everyone talked about the past and how much things had changed. Some talked about how they once had a large Sunday school, two Sunday services, and a variety of programs. Others talked about how the neighborhood around them had become increasingly more diverse in culture, language, and economic status. Their pain in the face of all the loss and change they had experienced was palpable, their sadness and despair visible. Their guilt and anger simmered in their tense and somewhat defensive words.

I asked what the congregation had done to reach out to their new neighbors.

"We've tried. But they're not interested in us," one man responded, an edge in his voice.

We spent the next several minutes talking about ways the congregation might reach out more effectively to their neighbors. When they asked about attracting families, we talked about hosting after-school programs for the children, offering classes for the parents, and using their large, mostly empty facility as a community center. We discussed redeveloping the congregation with a new name, new personality, and new mission focus. I thought there was some energy in the room.

But finally, one woman shook her head and said firmly, "But you don't understand, Pastor. We're old, we're tired, and we're done."

"Then, do you plan to close the congregation?" I asked honestly.

With one, angry voice, they said, "*No!*"

"Then what?" There was more defensiveness in my voice than I had intended. Didn't they understand that they needed to do something different to move forward?

The truth was ... they couldn't see it. Their grief was blocking their vision.

As I got to know this congregation over the next several years, I realized that when they said they were done, they didn't really mean it. What they really meant was that they felt trapped in their sadness and despair, guilt and anger, and fears and uncertainty about the future. Previous pastoral leaders had told them there was nothing they could do to "save" their congregation, and that left their spirits crushed and hopeless. They didn't know what to do and felt like everything I suggested had been tried or wouldn't work. They always had a reason, but many times it was just a rationalization of their reticence about trying anything new. They felt overwhelmed by the changes that swirled around them, guilty about what had happened to their once-thriving congregation, and powerless to do anything about it. They knew they needed to do something different, but though they couldn't say why, the prospect of change terrified them.

They were suffering from what psychologist Avery Wiseman calls "middle knowledge"—both knowing and not knowing at the same time—a common reaction before much grief work has been done.[17] They both knew and didn't know what they had lost. Intellectually they could describe what had happened to the congregation, but they were not able to fully articulate—to recognize—what those losses meant for the life and ministry of their congregation.

CONGREGATIONS AS EMOTIONAL SYSTEMS

In order to understand how a congregation is both influenced by and contributes to the experience of loss, it's helpful to think about how congregations function as "emotional systems," that is, a network of relationships shaped by emotional interactions and patterns of behavior.

A congregation is often referred to as a "family of faith" and the functioning of a congregation is frequently compared to the way family systems operate. While congregations are not families, the insights of family systems theory can help us appreciate how the reality of loss shapes a congregation's sense of itself and its ministry.[18]

Emotional relationships within a family affect the individual members' thoughts, feelings, and actions to the point that they can feel like they share a single "emotional skin."[19] The study of families as "emotional systems" has helped us understand how emotional interactions within a family influence and shape how the family responds and reacts as a unit to the broad range of experiences, events, and realities they face in their life together.[20]

Similar to families, congregations are systems where people interact with one another on an emotional level. One could paraphrase Jesus's words in Matthew 18, spoken in a discussion about dealing with conflict and forgiveness, to say, "Wherever two or three are gathered in my name, emotions

will result." Within the life of the congregation people experience joy, comfort, support, cooperation, and friendship
with one another. But they also experience anxiety, disagreement, frustration, anger, and defensiveness.[21] Over time,
these relationships and the emotional content that defines
them result in evolving patterns of behavior, practice, tradition, and conflict that mark a congregation's personality and
functioning.

Peter Steinke writes, "The church is more than its emotional processes, but it is never less than those processes."[22]
What this means is that the emotions at play within the life
of a congregation affect all the relationships and interactions
of the people within the congregation. This, in turn, affects
the way the congregation makes decisions, approaches planning, carries out activities, and understands the way things
are done in the congregation. This emotional impact can
intensify when a congregation is facing loss and the grief that
accompanies it. As we saw in chapter 2, grief is more than an
emotional response, including physical, behavioral, and spiritual reactions, but as Steinke suggests, our response to grief is
never less than the emotions it generates.

In a family system, individual members can respond to
loss differently. This can cause stress and conflict within the
family system. Following the death of a child, one parent's
expression of grief can be difficult for their partner to understand or appreciate, and this can result in tension and a sense
of estrangement between the couple.[23]

Like families, each congregation has its own way of being
in the world. Because the relationships within the life of each
congregation are different, each congregation will have its
own unique emotional system that shapes how it reacts and
responds to change, loss, and grief. Not only is each congregational system unique, but like individuals and families, each

congregation will respond and react differently during times of stress than in periods of calm.[24]

Unlike families, congregations are more fluid and the relationships less intense than those found within most families. Individuals move in and out of the congregational system, and their relationship to the congregation is, for the most part, voluntary. Beyond the "active core" of the congregation's membership, the connection individuals have with the life of the congregation may be very limited. All the individuals who make up congregations bring their own "baggage" with them, however, and that baggage affects everyone connected to the congregation. As people move in and out of the congregation over time, they bring along their experiences from other congregations, the patterns for dealing with grief and loss from the families they are a part of, their professional and vocational perspectives, cultural background, and a host of other experiences and characteristics that make them unique. Each individual brings along his or her own personal stories, experiences of loss, emotional maturity, and personality quirks. The fluidity and different levels of involvement within a congregation and the voluntary nature of congregational belonging make the emotional system of a congregation more complex than within the life of a family.

As you work through the experience of change, loss, and grief within the life in your congregation, it is important to be aware of and attend to the unique relationships and emotional responses that are at work in the congregational system. A relative newcomer will react to turning a former Sunday school room into an office for the local food pantry much differently from someone who remembers teaching in that room when his children were small. A person with a business background who serves on the finance committee is going to respond to the departure of a pastor differently from the person whose primary experience of the pastor was

74

her care and compassion as his spouse was dying. Some people will react to a loss with a loud voice; others will suffer in silence. As the losses associated with decline mount up, some members will be quick to cast blame, while others want time to think things through. Some will immediately want to find solutions and fix problems, while others will separate themselves from the congregation rather than deal with the losses. All these different responses can be difficult to understand, and managing them can be challenging. Conflict is inevitable.

In Conversation

In the first chapter, you shared some of your experiences with grief and loss. Think back on those conversations and what you shared.

- How might your personal experiences with loss and grief inform or get in the way of your response to change and loss in your congregation?
- How might your own story affect the way you view the church's story?

A CULTURE OF LOSS

While a congregation is made up of unique individuals who bring their experiences to bear in the life of the congregation and react and respond differently to change and loss, the congregational system itself can shape the way individuals respond to the losses incurred by the congregation. The relationship system within the congregation is not built out of the personalities of its members like blocks in a wall, but rather it is a network of interlocking relationships that affect one another, more like the strands in an intricate spider's web, bringing out certain aspects of individuals' personalities.

Whether it is recognized or not, congregations, like families, have a "culture of loss" that has developed over the course

75

of its history. Depending on the age of the congregation, this culture of loss can span generations as generations of members have been shaped by the losses they've experienced and worked through them in both healthy and unhealthy ways.

Family-focused grief therapy is an approach to palliative care[25] and bereavement that takes seriously the emotional system of a family and how it shapes a family's response to terminal illness and the grief following a loved one's death.[26] This family-focused approach involves actively assessing families as systems, harnessing their strengths and increasing their ability to cope adaptively with loss and grief.[27] Like our understanding of family systems in general, the insights and approach of family-focused grief therapy are applicable to congregations experiencing loss and grief. Family-focused grief therapy considers three dimensions of family functioning—cohesiveness, communication, and conflict—that define a family's culture of loss and how they respond (with reason and thoughtfulness) and react (more instinctively) to loss and grief as a system.[28] These three dimensions of family functioning reflect how easily the family system can adapt to the reality of loss and find a "new normal" in their life together. Families that are flexible, communicate well, work through conflict creatively, and deal with loss and grief in healthy and life-giving ways are known as "adaptive families." Understanding how these three dimensions function within a congregation's culture of loss can provide insight into the health and vitality of a congregation as it confronts changes, addresses loss, and works through the grief that loss can bring.

COHESIVENESS

Cohesiveness describes an emotional system's ability to function together as a team. This dimension of a family or congregation's system is the most powerful factor in determining how the system will respond to and work together in the face of loss.[29] As a congregation faces challenges, including those associated with decline and loss, congregations, like families, can be enmeshed, disengaged, or flexible.

As congregations experience decline and the resulting losses, they frequently become more and more enmeshed, turning inward and adopting a siege mentality focused solely on survival. These congregations value togetherness, describe themselves as a family, and often express their appreciation for how close and caring they are for one another. They often feel dismay when newcomers don't return or do not stay long. "We're so caring," members say. "How could they not want to be a part of that?" While being a caring community needs to be at the core of a congregation that strives to live out Jesus's gospel of compassion, forgiveness, mercy, and love, a congregation's care for one another can bind them so tightly to one another that it becomes impermeable to outsiders. A visitor to a small, enmeshed congregation once told me they felt like they were "crashing someone's family reunion." Another said that their experience was akin to "driving down the block, picking out a house at random, walking in, and trying to join the family for dinner."

Empty pews, aging membership, and shrinking finances generate fear and anxiety within the congregation.[30] In turn, fear and anxiety move us to cling to one another for a sense of security and safety. But fear and anxiety can also lead us to build protective walls that are difficult for others to climb, let alone find the entrance door. It can even be hard for a new pastor to permeate these walls and prevent the pastor from providing leadership for the struggling community. As the congregation struggles to maintain control, they can be suspicious and sometimes openly hostile to outsiders, especially outsiders who tell them what they should do.

As a congregation turns inward to protect themselves against further loss, the opposite generally happens: losses increase. In an attempt to defend the status quo, the enmeshed congregation will refuse to risk considering new ideas or approaches to ministry, especially if those ideas come from newcomers. They cling to one another like survivors of a sunken ship adrift in a lifeboat too fearful of sharks to wave their hands at rescue ships passing by on the horizon. Rather than accept the reality of their losses and acknowledge their grief, these congregations view loss as a threat to be avoided and express their grief by casting blame and anger at those outside their enmeshed system.

On the other end of the spectrum are congregations that respond to loss by disengaging from one another. Rather than clinging together for safety, members of these congregations distance themselves from one another. In these congregations, as the impact of multiple losses builds up, it becomes harder and harder to find people to step up and take responsibility for the life of the congregation. The result is that fewer and fewer people are tasked with more and more of the work. Leadership positions go unfilled as people remove themselves from being active members.

I remember a congregation where the lawn had gotten so long the city gave them a citation. No one in the congregation was willing to cut the grass. They didn't feel like they had the funds to hire someone to do it. The congregational meeting to address the issue was a difficult one as people reminisced about the days when they had a property committee to handle things like the lawn, and the money to properly care for their building and grounds. Eventually, one family agreed to cut half the lawn, and another reluctantly agreed to do the other half.

Unlike an enmeshed congregation, where it may be difficult for a pastor to penetrate the system and provide leadership, in a disengaged congregation, the pastor might be expected to pick up the slack left by disengaged members and is criticized when things formerly done by those members get left undone. One pastor of a disengaged congregation was expected to plan the annual vacation Bible school when no one in the congregation was found to coordinate the program. Another led the annual stewardship campaign when no one volunteered for the stewardship committee. Both were criticized because they didn't do things "the way they used to be done" by lay leaders.

Another sign of a disengaged congregation is the loss of members who choose to go elsewhere or no place at all as the realities of loss begin to take their toll on the life of the faith community. In a consumer culture where people choose a church based on whether it can meet their needs, rather than a commitment to the community and to the relationships that form that community, who could blame them? I mean, if my regular grocery store is out of root beer, I don't go without root beer out of loyalty to the store until it shows up. I simply go to the grocery store down the block and buy it there. But in a church community where we use metaphors like "family" and "body" to understand who we are, that kind of disengagement can itself create loss upon loss and add to the spiral of the pain of grief already present in the system.

Like the enmeshed congregation, a disengaged congregation often fails to deal with the losses they have experienced. Rather than viewing loss as a threat and adopting a siege mentality, the disengaged congregation tries to ignore the reality of the loss by putting their collective heads in the sand. Disengaged congregations are unable to take responsibility for their situation. Sometimes this is because they are "burned out," and sometimes it's because no one has ever equipped them to creatively respond to the losses they have experienced. Individuals expect someone else will figure it out for them. They may ask for denominational leaders to come in to "fix" their problems with money or other resources. They search for "silver parachutes" like bequests or benefactors to rescue them or prolong the status quo for a bit longer and for "silver bullet" solutions that will restore the glory days in one fell swoop.

In a flexible family, members recognize and respond to loss and grief in a healthy manner—by sharing their distress with one another, tolerating both positive and negative feelings, and providing support to one another. The family allows people to mourn at their own speed, and members willingly take on appropriate roles and complete necessary tasks.[31] A flexible family doesn't seek to assign blame, try to re-create the past, or find quick fixes for the complex challenges and changes it faces.

While enmeshed and disengaged congregations have a hard time accepting their losses and acknowledging their grief, "flexible congregations" are much better suited to face loss and express their grief. A flexible congregation both recognizes the importance of caring for one another within the family of faith and understands the need to reach out to love the neighbor beyond the church doors. It not only welcomes newcomers but also recognizes and welcomes the gifts and perspectives that they bring to the life of the congregation. In a flexible congregation, pastoral leaders are seen as partners in ministry and work alongside lay leaders in guiding the life of the congregation. A flexible congregation seeks to understand its context and adapt its ministry to that context. It recognizes what it has lost, understands the need to grieve, and uses its memories of the past as a source of wisdom to adapt to the present and build a vision for the future. In part 3 we will look at specific ways a congregation can become more adaptive in addressing loss and making changes to embrace God's future by drawing the best from their past.

In Conversation

In reality, most congregations lie on a continuum between being fully enmeshed and fully disengaged from one another. Flexible congregations tend to lie somewhere in the middle of the spectrum.

- Find a room with plenty of space.

- Place a chair with the word *enmeshed* on one side of the room and another with *disengaged* on the other side. Imagine a line connecting the two chairs.

- Have members of your group stand between the two chairs indicating where they think the congregation lands on the continuum. Then ask:

  - Why did you choose to stand where you did? What do you see in the functioning of the congregation that led you to that particular spot?

  - How does the place where you are standing reflect the way the congregation deals with loss?

COMMUNICATION

Adaptive congregational systems, like adaptive family systems, communicate in a way that fosters an openness with one another and an honest disclosure of thoughts and feelings.[32] These expressive congregations share their problems, feel free to disagree, and are comfortable conveying both positive and negative feelings with one another. Communication is the most important tool a congregation has for dealing with loss and grief. Good communication skills and practices contribute to healthy cohesion and help to mitigate conflict when it arises.

Good communication is only partly about being aware of our thoughts and feelings and expressing them clearly and respectfully. Good communication also requires skilled active listening. A good deal of my time involved in the pastoral care of bereaved persons was spent listening. Being able to tell one's story of loss and grief is critical to the healing process,

81

but a storyteller needs someone to listen. We need to be willing to listen to one another's stories, understanding that another person's experience of loss within the congregation may not be the same as our own. Not everyone will feel concern over the decline in finances the way the treasurer does. Not everyone will understand why the congregation's failure to get the grass cut is a bigger deal than just getting a warning from the city. Not everyone will feel the same way about the loss of the Sunday school, or the inability to pay the pastor. In one congregation, some members expressed their opinion that paying the mortgage and keeping their building was more important than paying a pastor. Others vehemently disagreed, arguing that they should sell their building and use the money to pay the pastor. It wasn't easy for the two sides to listen to one another, but listening well was critically important for them to address the potential losses they were facing without splintering the congregation.

Throughout this book, you have been and will continue to be asked to tell each other stories about your experiences of loss in your own life and in the life of the congregation. These exercises are not only intended to help you develop a common sense of who you are and where you have been as a congregation, but also to practice listening to one another and your various and possibly divergent perspectives. Grief needs to be shared, or it will come out in unhealthy ways. Swallowing grief can lead to physical ailments like headaches, stomach problems, insomnia, and a host of other illnesses. Unexpressed strong emotions cause people to act out in ways that are sometimes hurtful and destructive.

I know of a congregation that rarely kept a pastor beyond a year or two because they had never come to terms with a previous pastor's sexual misconduct. It took a wise new pastor to finally help them make the connection. When she gave them permission to talk, out loud, about his misconduct and express the grief and pain they felt because of his actions, they were able to work through their feelings of betrayal, loss, and anger, and reestablish trust in their leader. After those conversations, the pastor was able to serve there for many years.

Expressive congregations are not only open to discussing their losses among themselves, but they are also open to seeking help from others. They look for and welcome outside sources of ideas and guidance. Denominational leaders are often willing and able to help a congregation address their experiences. Congregations that are struggling with similar issues and those that have already walked the path of grief and have found a way forward can be consulted. Coaches and consultants can be hired. Books (like this one) can be read. Prayer asking for the guidance of the Holy Spirit is extremely important. There is no shame in asking for help. God put us in communities for a reason!

Creating spaces in the congregation's schedule to provide opportunities for open, honest, and expressive communication, and making places available where people feel safe to share their thoughts and feelings is critical when dealing with loss and throughout the grief process. Naming the losses we have experienced can help us deal with them in the light of day rather than allowing them to sneak up on us from the shadows.

In Conversation

Practice listening to one another! Many active listening exercises are available online. Here's a simple one.

- Divide into pairs.
- One person tells a brief story (one to two minutes) about something that happened this past week. It can be about anything.
- The other person listens and then repeats the story back to the storyteller.
- The first person should correct any inaccuracies or point out any key details that are missing. Then, switch roles.
- After the exercise discuss: How does this simple exercise reflect what can happen in the life of the congregation?

CONFLICT

Dealing with the effects of change and the experience of loss can often result in conflict within the congregation.[33] Consider the congregation in the last section that felt they had to decide between paying a pastor and keeping their building. The loss of financial capacity resulted in conflict, as difficult decisions and choices needed to be made. A new pastor who quickly makes changes, even necessary ones, can touch off significant pushback and division as people react to the perceived losses the changes will bring. An influx of new members can lead to conflict with long-term members as the newcomers move into leadership positions, resulting in the long-term members losing roles or power within the congregational system.

Conflict can create a great deal of stress and anxiety in the system, especially if it is not dealt with openly and honestly. But, in some congregations, dealing openly and honestly with conflict can be a real problem. Somewhere we got the idea that Christians should never disagree with one another, should never argue, or have differences of perspective or opinion. Many congregations suffer from this "Niceness Syndrome." Niceness Syndrome drives conflict underground and covers it over with an artificial veneer that makes everything seem just fine. Certainly, if the church were without sin, it might be conflict-free. But we are not, so disagreements, arguments, and differences of opinion and perspective do happen within congregations. In a congregation suffering from Niceness Syndrome, this conflict often comes out in passive-aggressive and very destructive ways.

The Scriptures are full of stories of conflict but are also filled with wisdom for working through our conflicts with one another. In Matthew 18, Jesus gives his disciples advice and counsel on dealing with conflict within the community of faith. He promises that he will be with them in the midst of their disagreements and encourages them to forgive one another "seventy times seven" and to work at reconciliation for as long as it takes.

As conflict intensifies within a congregation, tongues loosen, ears close, and communication begins to break down. As the book of James says, "How great a forest is set ablaze by a small fire! And the tongue is a fire" (3:5–6). As conflict ramps up, people begin to take up and defend positions rather than work toward mutually beneficial solutions. They dig foxholes and gather like-minded members to their cause. They identify scapegoats and look for people to blame. Cohesion breaks down as people distance themselves from one another or leave the congregation altogether. Communication deteriorates as leaders try to control the flow of information, and conversations move from the council room to the parking lot to "secret" meetings in people's living rooms. As cohesion and communication decline, anxiety and fear deepen, resulting in further losses. Divisions can result in further loss of leadership, income, and resources. Roles and relationships are damaged, creating secondary losses. Loss of friendships due to disagreement or departure adds to the unresolved grief already in the system. Typically, one party or the other eventually "wins," a truce is called, and niceness settles on the congregation, driving the issues and concerns back underground. But the truce is temporary. The grief and pain of the loss caused by the conflict are never dealt with and come out again down the road as the cycle of loss, anxiety, division, and conflict repeats itself.

Highly conflicted families are the least effective in dealing with loss and grief. These hostile families are fractured and chaotic. Family members refuse to talk with one another. Continual arguments destroy teamwork and damage the ability of the family to provide support for one another. Conflicted families are least able to make use of resources and social support in the face of loss and often have poor coping strategies, which prevents them from working through their grief.[34]

In a similar way, highly conflicted congregations find it difficult to deal with losses that spark disagreement or division. Grief can exacerbate and draw out already-existing divisions and bring out old disagreements. Unresolved grief, unexpressed anger, and hurt feelings can be held in the collective memory of the congregation and resurface during subsequent times of tension or when the congregation is confronted with new losses.

To be clear, not all conflict is bad. Conflict becomes unhealthy only when we don't deal with it openly, honestly, and directly. Conflict becomes problematic when we allow it to divide us, become defensive with one another, and vilify those we disagree with. But a certain level of disagreement and difference of opinion is healthy and even necessary for a congregation to be creative in its mission and ministry and to meet the challenges it faces. I strongly believe that different perspectives rubbing up against each other make for ideas, programs, solutions, and adaptations that are better thought out and stronger. A moderate level of conflict is a normal part of growth. Researcher David Roozen found that congregations with some minor conflict grew at a higher rate than those with no conflict and considerably faster than those with serious conflict.[35]

The difference between a healthy and unhealthy system is not to be found in the presence or absence of conflict. While we have seen that high levels of conflict reflect dysfunctionality within a system, a total lack of conflict may also reflect dysfunctionality. Adaptive family systems are not without conflict any more than healthy congregations are always nice. Instead, adaptive families and congregations possess an ability to resolve conflict creatively and in ways that are mutually beneficial to those who are involved.

This ability to use conflict creatively is grounded in a family or congregation's flexible cohesion and expressive communication. Families and congregations that are able to use conflict creatively are able to see the value in differences of opinion and perspective, meet each other with respect, and see each other first as beloved children of God, created in God's image.

In Conversation

- How has conflict played a role in the life of your community of faith?
- How have your congregation's cohesion patterns and communication styles contributed to or become barriers to your recognizing, acknowledging, and understanding the losses you have faced as a congregation?

In this chapter, we have considered the external and internal factors that have contributed to the changes and resulting losses that many congregations are experiencing today. External factors like changes in social participation, including involvement in religious communities, and patterns of belonging have resulted in losses in membership and, in turn, the loss of human and financial resources for doing ministry. Internally, these losses cause imbalance in congregational emotional systems, resulting in a loss of meaning, sense of order and predictability, changed or lost relationships, and an increase in anxiety. Congregations respond to these losses in a variety of ways that can get in the way of dealing with loss, contribute to further losses, or facilitate accepting the reality of the grief, depending on the level of cohesion, communication, and conflict in the congregation's system. Accepting the reality of these losses calls forth the reactions and responses of grief within the life of the congregation.

In the next chapter we will explore further how congregations respond and react to the experience of grief, and take a deeper look at our yearning and how we try in vain to re-create that which has been lost.

BIBLE STUDY: 1 CORINTHIANS 1:18–31

1. Read 1 Corinthians 1:18–31.

2. We have been discussing factors both outside and inside the congregation that contribute to the losses we have experienced and our reaction to those losses. Based on your discussions, consider the following questions. (There is no one "right" answer here. Pick the one that resonates with you, and share why with your group.)

a. How does the "foolishness of the cross" that Paul writes about speak to our experience of loss?

1. The cross reminds us that loss is a part of life.

88

2. The cross shows us that God stands with us in our experience of loss.

3. Jesus's death on the cross was far worse than any loss we've experienced.

4. God is more powerful than any loss we face.

b. Paul says that God chooses to work through what is foolish, weak, low, and despised in the world so that no one may boast in God's presence (vv. 27–31). What does this say to us as we think about the losses we have experienced?

1. When we are at our lowest, that's when God can do God's best work.

2. Our experience of loss can help us remember what is really important in ministry.

3. Loss can "take us down a few notches" when we think too highly of ourselves.

4. God can use the world around us, even with all the changes, to teach us something.

A Scrapbook of Memories: The Grief Response

All people are grass,

their constancy is like the flower of the field. (Isa 40:6)

The pastoral candidate followed the council president through the small, rural church. As they walked together, the gray-haired farmer shared the history of his congregation. He stopped by a long thick rope that dangled from the ceiling in the narrow entryway, giving it a half-hearted tug. "Doesn't work anymore," he said, a hint of sadness in his voice. "The bell broke. Maybe ten years ago. We didn't have the money to fix it." He gave a short laugh. More of a grunt, really. "I remember my daughter being pulled off her feet by the recoil when she was an acolyte. The kids all thought it was fun."

"How old is your daughter?" the pastor asked.

"She's thirty-five. Her own daughter is about the same age she was back then. We don't see them in church much."

They walked into the sanctuary and down the narrow aisle.

Each stained-glass window had a small gold plate attached to the bottom of the metal frame. They paused before each window so the pastor could read the name of the donor etched into the metal and the president could share a memory. "Took us five years to collect the funds for all the windows. Farm prices were down, and people were struggling. But we got it done!" There was pride in his voice, then the sadness returned. "Most of those families are gone now. Kids moved away. Things have changed a lot since then."

The tour continued up steep steps to the balcony. A row of dusty boxes marked "choir robes" filled the back pews. "I remember one Sunday when the pastor had to stop the sermon and straighten out a bunch of us boys who were screwing around up here. There wasn't a choir that week. . . . Don't remember why not." The lines beside the man's blue-gray eyes crinkled with genuine laughter. "Of course, nobody sits up here anymore. As you can see, we mostly use it for storage."

Down again.

In the basement fellowship hall, the president stopped by an old, rotating photo display that held confirmation pictures behind yellowed, cracking plastic panes. He turned it slowly, studying the black-and-whites of large groups of junior high students in their white robes. "There's my daughter." He pointed to a girl with long, straight hair and black plastic-rimmed glasses. He flipped several more boards. He pointed to a young man with a brush haircut wearing a black robe in a group of eight. "That's me. It wasn't long after the church was built."

They walked through the fellowship hall, a tired room with well-worn floor tiles and paint peeling from the cinder block. "Had my wedding reception here," he said. "And both my parents' funeral dinners." He paused for a moment to look at a faded painting of Jesus the Good Shepherd. "We have a lot more funeral dinners than wedding receptions these days."

They ascended the back stairs to the outside door, walked through the church's yard, and crossed the street to the church cemetery. For the next hour, the president introduced the pastor to the matriarchs and patriarchs, family members and friends of the congregation who lay buried there. Each gravestone held a story. Several children were interred there too. A sickness. A farm accident. A stillbirth.

For long-time members, a church building is a three-dimensional scrapbook of memories. Each picture, each room, and each corner holds a memory of days gone by, relationships past and present, and a reminder how things used to be. The bricks and mortar that surround the congregation each Sunday tell the story of what it has lost. Like the prophet Isaiah's words to the people in exile, the building itself can remind us that we are like grass and flowers that whither and fade and die. But it's not just the long-time members who value a building's stories. Even newer members can make powerful associations with the bricks and mortar, depending on their experiences in the community of faith and what first brought them to the congregation.

The scrapbook of memories held in your church building and grounds can reinforce the sense of yearning for the way things used to be in your congregation. A congregation clings to an old hymnal because it links worshipers to a time in their past, perhaps one now lost. The familiar hymns remind them of childhood, young adulthood, or a seemingly "simpler" time when the church was as a church should be, and the world outside the doors was more understandable. The faded old banners connect long-time members to the ones who lovingly made them in the basement of the church and to a time when people had the time to gather together to work on projects like that. The boxes of dated, worn choir robes are still kept in the balcony, waiting for the day when the choir comes back.

In Conversation

Take a tour of your congregation's "scrapbook of memories."

- Walk slowly through the sanctuary and narthex.
- Reflect on the worship services you've attended and the people you've shared those spaces with over the years.
- Wander down the halls and through the classrooms.
- What memories do those places bring to mind?
- Stand in the fellowship hall and remember the gatherings you have experienced there.
- Even more, try to notice the feelings and thoughts those spaces generate in you.
- How do you physically react to the memories that are evoked?
- Did this walk spur any memories that need to be added to your timeline?

In the last chapter, we considered the importance of accepting the reality of the losses that come to us as the world around us and the congregation itself changes. Until losses are recognized, it is easy to rationalize or dismiss them and postpone or avoid necessary mourning.[1] If something gets in the way of working on this first task of grief, it becomes very difficult to address the other tasks in the grief process. Unfortunately, in most congregations, there is no body to bury, just empty pews, reduced finances, and deteriorating buildings to lament. Because these losses often come slowly over time, they are not always consciously acknowledged as losses. Instead they just feel like gnawing irritations that no one seems able to fix, like a stone in your shoe that you just can't get rid of. In some cases, the grief reactions caused by the pain of loss are clear and unmistakable, like our sadness at discontinuing a Sunday school program. At other times grief comes out in places where we least expect it, and seldom do we recognize these reactions as related to grief—for example, our anger at singing an unfamiliar hymn, or our negative reaction to a new pastor's way of doing things. Some reactions occur at or near the surface of our life together, while others occur much deeper and in less tangible ways.

In Conversation

Think about your own scrapbook of memories and reflect on your timeline.

- What are some of the "stones in your congregation's shoe" that are the result of loss? Name them out loud.

Think about not only the obvious ones (which I have called "the litany of lament") but the less obvious ones as well.

Before we go further, I want to remind you that, like the losses connected to high school graduation we discussed in chapter 1, not all changes congregations face are negative. But even positive change can result in loss and lead to grief. Congregations that experience rapid growth, for example, can struggle with loss. It is hard to make the transition from a small, family-like church where everyone knows everyone to a larger, program-style church where the pastor might not even know everyone's name. The loss of the intimacy the congregation had when it was smaller can create ripples of discontent and frustration, grief and yearning for days gone by that, if left unaddressed, can cause difficulties in the life of the congregation. Growth can lead to members leaving to find more intimate communities of faith, resentment toward newcomers, or criticism of the pastor and staff for not being as available to long-time members. These difficulties can easily lead to conflict. While I have seen this growth-stimulated loss happen on a number of occasions, loss due to decline is a more common experience in congregations these days. For that reason, most of the discussion that follows will focus there. But we don't want to forget that situations other than decline can cause a grief response in congregations too.

RESPONDING TO GRIEF

It is one thing to accept the reality of our losses on an intellectual level; it is another to acknowledge it as loss, accept it on an emotional level, and work through the grief responses that acknowledgment may draw out within the community of faith. It is one thing to yearn for days gone by and another to come to the gut realization that those days are not coming back. It is one thing to recognize the tangible losses—after a while it is hard to ignore the empty pews Sunday after Sunday—but it's another to identify and explore the symbolic losses that can result from the tangible ones. At some point we will need to confront and deal with our grief and all the emotions and other reactions that come with it. But because the grief responses in a congregation can be complicated and the network of relationships complex, patience is called for. We need to be patient both with our brothers and sisters in the congregation and with ourselves. Once you start this work, you need to give yourself the time and space to see it through. ←

Rather than acknowledge the losses that come with the changes a congregation has experienced, congregations often try to avoid the emotional content of those losses and respond with rationalizations and other ways of avoiding their grief. At best, avoiding grief only defers and delays our reaction to it. At worst, grief will find its way out in unintended, unhealthy, and even destructive ways. Congregations can also respond to their grief indirectly by blaming people and circumstances for their losses, and by trying to re-create the past to restore their community of faith to its previous glory.

THE BLAME GAME

A common response to loss in congregations is to assign blame, looking for cause-and-effect relationships to explain away losses and put responsibility for those losses on scapegoats inside and outside of the congregation. Lack of youth and young families is blamed on soccer schedules and other activities. Members are blamed for irregular worship patterns and branded as being less than faithful. Empty pews are dismissed as "low Sundays," with the expectation that attendance will be better next week. I have been told many times that low attendance was due to the fact that "people were away" and that "we usually have more than this," only to be told in confidence later that they usually don't. An ineffective pastor or church conflict is often blamed for beginning a decline from which the congregation never recovered. Financial difficulties are blamed on fixed incomes or on the lack of generosity in "younger generations."

All of these explanations may have some truth in them. Soccer schedules do take youth and their families away on weekends. Ineffective pastors and congregational conflicts can drive people away. But these rationalizations make it easy to avoid the realities of the losses and create the illusion that they are problems that can be "fixed." If we just develop the right kind of youth program (one like we remember from years ago), we are sure the youth and their families would forgo soccer and come back to church. If we just got the "right" pastor, the congregation would grow. If we just brought in more members or ran the right stewardship campaign, the finances would improve. I've seen congregations struggle mightily to do all these things, usually with disappointing results.

As we have seen, all of these changes are not the result of single causes, but a variety of factors both internal and external to the life of the congregation. External events and trends may have led to the losses the congregation has experienced, but internal responses, or the lack of response to those external issues, may have exacerbated the losses or resulted in secondary losses. Understanding this mutual interplay of factors provides a more accurate, and therefore more helpful, picture of the dynamics that have resulted in the losses the congregation is experiencing.[2]

The advantage of considering and addressing this mutual interplay of factors, rather than searching for simple cause and effect, can be illustrated in the story of a couple I knew a number of years ago. They had recently left the congregation I was serving and moved to a new community. The young woman told me they had given up trying to find a church home there, because they were tired of being treated like "prey" in the congregations they visited. "We have decided we can just worship God on our own," she said matter-of-factly. It was also clear that being part of a congregation was something she considered good, even preferable to not belonging—but ultimately saw belonging to a congregation as optional for the life of faith.

Before moving to their new community this woman and her husband had been quite active in the ministry where I was serving. During their time in our congregation, they had served as worship leaders and were regular participants in Bible studies and involved in service ministries. Like many people in our consumer-based society, they were looking for a community of faith where their spiritual needs would be met. The congregations they visited, however, were looking for young adults who could help them save their declining church and help them preserve their way of doing things. Neither found what they were looking for. It would have been easy for each to blame the other for this couple's failure to find and join a congregation. Neither the couple nor the congregations realized they were caught up in a web of

97

unrecognized and unacknowledged influences that each contributed to this couple choosing not to be a part of any congregation. They eventually did find a congregation to join. The couple chose the congregation because members seemed more interested in getting to know and understand them and the world where they lived than figuring out how to use them to sustain their declining community.

RE-CREATING THE PAST

ISN'T GOING TO HAPPEN

Another common way congregations respond to change and its attendant losses is by trying to re-create the past. We remember when the ministry was thriving and convince ourselves that if we just did things more efficiently, or better, or worked harder, or had more commitment from members, things would turn around, the losses would be reversed, and things would return to "normal" (the way things used to be). Unfortunately attempts at resurrecting past glories almost never work.

In the preface, I talked about putting up posters in my first campus ministry to invite students to our worship services and said that no one responded to them. That wasn't the end of the story. Not ready to admit that the world of a university campus had changed since my student days, I decided the problem was with the posters. If I just made better posters, the students would come. So, the next week, I used brighter paper and tried to give the posters a more "professional" look. Still, no one came. Then I decided I must be putting them up in the wrong places. So, the next week, I put up more posters in new places. Still no one came. Honestly? I could have wallpapered the campus with posters, and it wouldn't have mattered. Just doing the same things better will not help re-create a past that has been lost. It took me a while, but I finally recognized that and began looking for new ways to reach students.

As we saw in the last chapter, in the face of destabilizing experiences of loss, congregations can turn inward while trying to maintain "normalcy" as much as possible. When customary patterns are disturbed in a congregational system, the system will work to reduce the shock on the system by attempting to restore the familiar or making things "the same as they were back in . . ."[3] (you can fill in the blank). Clinging to traditions, written and unwritten rules about how things should be done, and familiar ways of doing things can be a coping mechanism that helps the community deal with the imbalance, uncertainty, anxiety, and confusion of change and loss, at least for a while. But as those once-effective traditions, rules, and time-worn ways of doing things continue to break down, frustration, anger, resistance, and conflict can develop as the reality of the changes becomes apparent. To move forward, at some point the congregation needs to acknowledge the sobering reality that re-creating the past is no more likely than bringing a loved one back from the grave. Once that begins to set in, the pain of grief is soon to follow.

In Conversation

- How do your congregation's traditions, written and unwritten rules, and ways of doing things help you to cope with the changes and losses you've experienced?
- How might they be getting in the way of acknowledging and expressing your losses?

EXPERIENCING OUR GRIEF

Acknowledging and understanding the losses your congregation has experienced, even on an emotional level, only gets you partway to coming to terms with them. It is not enough to say "Yep, we've lost all those things" and then just set them aside as if they didn't matter, though Lord knows we try to do that sometimes! As we come to accept the reality of what we have lost, we begin to work on the second task of the grief process, "processing the pain of the grief."[4] This task involves expressing our grief in the wide variety of ways it can manifest itself in us and in the life of the congregation. Grief, we need to remember, is more than just an emotion. It is a complex set of responses and reactions that can express themselves in psychological, physical, behavioral, and spiritual ways.

The only way through grief is to grieve. This cannot be said often enough. Attempting to avoid grief or deal with it indirectly simply doesn't work. To find our way through the grief process, we need to directly address the range of responses grief can generate in our congregational systems and in us personally. While each experience of grief is unique, we can identify some common responses and reactions that we can anticipate, learn to recognize, and be prepared to work through as we consider the losses we have identified. Anxiety and yearning are two of the most common grief responses in congregational life, along with the more familiar emotions associated with grief: sadness, despair, guilt, and anger.

ANXIETY

Anxiety is one of the first and most basic grief reactions to change and loss both in our individual lives and in the corporate life of a congregation. Because everything in our church buildings can remind us in subtle and not-so-subtle ways that things aren't the way they used to be, the scrapbook of memories that surrounds us each Sunday morning can generate feelings of anxiety within and among us. The effect of empty pews, bells that no longer work, and pictures of days gone by can subconsciously gnaw away at our hearts and our souls. When systems are stressed, pressured, or disrupted by internal or external forces, anxiety results.[5]

All relationship systems, including families and congregations, become anxious. It is inevitable when you put people together.[6] Change and loss, because it upsets the stable balance in a congregational system, is one of the leading causes of anxiety in congregational life. Anxiety is sometimes confused with fear, but they are different. Fears have a definite focus. Congregations can be afraid they cannot pay the bills because the balance in their checkbook is too low or afraid families will leave because there is no longer a youth group or afraid the congregation won't be there when it comes time for their funeral. Anxiety is more of a free-floating sense of awkwardness and unease. It's often hard to put your finger on the source of it. It creates a tension, uncomfortableness, and dis-ease within the community that visitors may pick up on more quickly than those who are in the midst of it week in and week out.

However, like leaves swirling in a fall wind, anxiety will eventually settle somewhere. Peter Steinke writes, "Relationship systems have favorite ducts and crevices for the deposit of [anxiety's] flow."[7] Like leaves collecting in the rain gutters, the anxiety often finds its way to the most vulnerable or responsible people in the system. The targets for the anxiety in a congregational system often include pastors, elders, council members, musicians, secretaries, administrators, and other leaders. It can focus on a large influx of newcomers or those in the congregation who are in some way different from the majority. This settling anxiety may result in a vague sense of unease at "all the changes" going on or develop into a full-blown fear that the long-term members will be neglected by the pastor in favor of the newcomers.

In Conversation

Look back over your timeline.

- When have you experienced high levels of anxiety in your congregation? Perhaps you are right now.
- Mark times of high anxiety on the timeline.
- Try to identify and discuss where anxiety tends to land in your congregation.
- How has this anxiety been manifest?
- How have you dealt with it?

Anxiety is a natural reaction to the disequilibrium that is caused by change and loss. It is a symptom, not the disease. Like a fever tells us that something is wrong with the body, anxiety can warn us that something is out of sync in the congregational system and needs our attention. If acknowledged and addressed, anxiety can provoke change and push us toward innovation.[8] If left unacknowledged and unaddressed, anxiety can manifest itself in irritability, restlessness, and a simmering sense of panic that sometimes bubbles over in reactive behaviors and rash decisions that, from the outside, seem to defy logic.

I've seen congregations eliminate parts of their music ministry to save money and then wonder why worship attendance has dropped. I've seen congregations lash out at members who propose new ways of doing ministry for fear that they might fail and make things worse. I've seen congregations welcome newcomers with open arms, invite them to get involved, and then get upset when they don't do things the way the congregation has always done them. I heard a story once about a newcomer who was dismissed from the church kitchen because she cut a pan of bars the wrong way! When there is anxiety in the congregation, it should not be dismissed as a problem of a few, but the leaders should listen carefully to determine what is going on behind the anxiety, ask what is driving the anxiety, and see how those deeper concerns might be addressed. Be aware that it could be caused by a sense of loss and its attending grief.

In many congregations that are experiencing decline, anxiety becomes chronic. Anxiety becomes the habitual state of the congregation and drives everything the congregation does and decides. As people react to the anxiety in the system, it creates polarities, which results in more anxiety and the cycle repeats itself. In time, this pattern is reinforced and maintained within the life of the congregation. Individuals become unbending and inflexible, staking out their positions, digging their foxholes to defend "their" church against further loss, and distancing themselves from and even vilifying whomever they have identified as the opposition. This results in more anxiety and reactivity, and the cycle continues.[9] In the end, this chronic cycle defeats anxiety's ability to alert us to the need for action and instead magnifies differences, constricts and limits congregational life, and diminishes our ability to think creatively. Like a fever, anxiety is good if attended to but can be highly destructive to the body if left unchecked.

The only way to break this cycle is to name it for what it is, identify those things that are driving it, and explore the emotions and reactions it is causing. Often those who bring the most anxiety with them to the congregation from home or work or some other aspect of their lives will be the most anxious people in the congregation. Rather than attacking people caught up in an anxiety cycle, arguing with them, or conceding to their reactivity, wise leaders offer care and compassion for these brothers and sisters. That can be challenging if you are the target of the anxious reactivity!

You cannot resolve chronic anxiety with more anxiety. That never works. As with any grieving person, gentleness, not judgment, is called for, along with an awareness and acknowledgment of the pain people are carrying in their hearts and souls. Through care-full listening, we need to be open to hearing one another's anxiety and exploring its roots together. Even before we do this listening, we need to be aware of and be able to name our own anxieties and how they are affecting our responses and reactions. If there is anxiety in the system, everyone, even the least anxious person in the system, will be affected by it to some extent.

YEARNING

Yearning is another common grief reaction. Preoccupied with the deceased, bereaved persons long to be reunited with the person who died. Frequently they report feeling an overwhelming sense of the lost loved one's presence in the room with them, even though no one can be seen. Mourners also regularly report talking with, experiencing being physically touched by, and even seeing their deceased loved one. Yearning can manifest itself in fantasies about the death not being real. The bereaved can weave stories about the person faking their death, being away on a trip, or having moved away. While the mourner knows intellectually that these stories are not true, they can bring a certain level of comfort and help the mourner cope with the early days of the loss. Yearning can cause the bereaved person to project their desire for reunion with the deceased onto others, including their children, friends, neighbors, acquaintances, or even strangers. The intensity of yearning can be experienced physically as well as emotionally. Mourners describe this yearning as "gut wrenching" or as a "heartache"—a literal pain in their chest—or as a "gnawing emptiness" that can't be filled.[10]

Different from nostalgia, yearning is characterized by obsessive rumination and a fixation on the past that paralyzes the mourner and makes it difficult to think about the future.

Persistent yearning can result in the mourner disengaging from their social world and "living in the past." Living backward provides a sense of continuity with the past and security in the present in a world where both feel permanently broken. As we saw in chapter 3, nostalgic thoughts and feelings have been shown to help someone to draw strength and encouragement from the past, whereas yearning traps one there.

Next to anxiety, yearning is one of the most frequently observed congregational responses to the loss of the past. Congregations can yearn for a particular time in their past; the ministry of a particular pastor; or a specific program, ministry, or event from days gone by. In the same way, pastors can yearn for a previous congregation and bring that loss with them into a new situation. A retired pastor once told me that there was always one call in a pastor's career that stood out as the "best of times" in a pastor's ministry. He knew exactly which of his calls had been the "best of times" for him and admitted trying to re-create that call in subsequent calls. Lay leaders and members can yearn for experiences in previous congregations too. As we have seen, trying to re-create the past is rarely, if ever, a successful strategy for congregational renewal. That is especially true when members of the congregation, the pastor, and others (such as denominational leaders) are all trying to re-create different pasts!

As with individuals who live in the past, yearning can cause a congregation to turn inward, disengage from their community, and distance themselves from denominational and ecumenical partners. Trapped in the past, individuals, groups, and even the whole congregation can become so narrowly fixed on the meaning, pleasure, and intimacy they remember from their "glory days" that they are unable to acknowledge their present reality or discern God's calling as they consider the future.

Like the mourner who fantasizes about the deceased loved one, congregations can create fantasies about their past that are not fully based in reality. The past can be scrubbed of the negativity, challenge, or struggle that almost certainly existed at the time. This unreality can further complicate the congregation's ability to look honestly and creatively at their present situation. Trying to re-create the remembered perfection of days gone by is impossible, if for no other reason than the fact that the perfection remembered probably never existed in the first place.

Finally, yearning for the past can cause a congregation to look at congregations that are doing "better" than they are (or that they think are doing "better") with jealousy and covetousness. The congregation down the block with a full parking lot, active youth program, and new building only underscores what they do not have and how things used to be. But when pushed on that one, they usually say that making the changes necessary to become more like their neighbors would just be too much. From their perspective, it would mean giving up their link to the past, which they are unwilling or unable to do. As a colleague of mine says, "They may want to want to change, but that's as far as it goes."

In Conversation

Look back at your timeline.

- If there was one event, ministry, or tradition you could re-create, what would it be?
- If there is one pastor you could bring back, who would it be?
- If there was one time in your past you would like to re-create, what would it be?

Consider why you yearn for these things.

- What was lost when things changed, were intentionally discontinued, or simply quit happening?
- Get behind the things themselves and ask what values, principles, strengths, or joys these things represent.
- Why did you find these things meaningful?
- How are these values, principles, strengths, or joys present in your ministry today?
- Brainstorm new ways they might be given new shape and form in your faith community.

THE PAIN OF GRIEF

In addition to the anxiety and yearning that the grief of change and loss can generate in a congregation, grief can also stimulate emotions like sadness, despair, guilt, and anger that dwell much closer to the surface. Sadness can lead to distancing and separating ourselves from the community, and despair can devolve further into a preoccupation with the past. Anger, the natural response to the deprivation of loss, can be redirected at the pastor, leadership, or others in the congregation. Guilt can be turned into blame or self-reproach. Sadness, despair, anger, and guilt as well as the range of other emotions that come from grief frequently involve pain.

Naturally, most of us would rather avoid pain if we can, and so we attempt to push these negative feelings away. Con-

107

gregations can adopt a number of conscious and unconscious strategies to avoid the pain caused by the changes they have experienced and their grief at the loss of their past. In spite of our desire to avoid it, the pain of loss and grief inevitably comes out, often emerging in unhealthy ways and resulting in poor communication, unresolved conflict, and a breakdown in the cohesion of the congregation.

Attempting to control a situation that seems uncontrollable is one of the most common ways of reacting to the pain of loss, though we often don't recognize it as a grief response. In a world of change and a sea of loss, even something small can bring grief to the surface. When things feel out of control and anxiety is high, little things can touch off a crisis. A friend of mine got into all sorts of trouble because he unwittingly put the Nativity scene in a different place the first Christmas in his new congregation. Members of the church council called the bishop and told him the pastor needed to go. I know how he felt. I got into trouble in one congregation because I rearranged things on the altar so I could reach them better and see the worship book more clearly. You would have thought I had banished Christ from the sanctuary! The altar guild didn't fully understand exactly why my actions upset them so much, but they did.

To be fair, my rearranging of the altar was motivated in part by my own need to control things in a new situation. That was also part of what was going on with the altar guild when they reacted so strongly to my rearranging the altar. When the stability and established patterns of a system are disrupted by loss, the system will work to reestablish the balance and restore the equilibrium—to control the unsettling change.[11] The need to control things, especially down to the tiniest detail, arises from an attempt to cover up the vulnerability and insecurity that results from change and loss.

Pastors and governing boards often struggle with each

other for control in anxious congregations experiencing decline. Individuals outside the formal power structure of the congregation can aggressively seek to take charge when things have become uncertain and chaotic and the change has become overwhelming. Often they try controlling things with threats of leaving or withdrawing financial support. In some congregations, where open conflict is not allowed, these attempts at taking control become passive aggressive and manifest themselves in individuals or groups undermining the pastor and formal leaders in a variety of unhealthy and destructive ways.

If unresolved grief is at the heart of these controlling behaviors—and it often is—things will not change until the grief and its pain have been confronted and worked through. Anxiety will grow and become more paralyzing. Anger and guilt will continue to be misdirected rather than being resolved. Sadness and despair will deepen, and hopelessness and helplessness will set in. An unwillingness to take risks for fear of losing what little stability they have will limit flexibility and adaptability in the congregation. The need to protect what is, rather than think creatively about what could be, solidifies the congregation's desire to keep things as they are.

This desire to keep things as they are is, at its root, about the need to control the uncontrollable. Remember Carol, whom we met in chapter 1, who was finally able to dust her son's room ten months after his death? Her deep fear was that if she changed her son's room in any way, she would forget him. She was terrified that if she even cleaned his room, his memory would disappear with the dust. A congregation's need to preserve the building, as well as familiar practices, patterns, traditions, and ways of doing things, comes from the same impetus. The unspoken fear is that the congregation will lose its identity, its sense of who it is, and in the face of decline, that identity may feel like the only thing the congregation has left.

Writing about an older person, bereaved of a long-time spouse, who is considering relocating from their home, William Worden writes, "One should never underestimate the importance of a home, where the bereaved may have lived for a long time and which may represent a whole scrapbook of meanings for the older person."[12] A new pastor, eager to move a congregation forward, who comes in and starts changing things around in a church building without understanding its symbolic and emotional meaning for the people who gather there, does so at their peril. I've seen it happen more than once. Change can happen; it probably even needs to happen. But to initiate change before understanding the scrapbook of memories in the walls is to neglect a barrier that cannot be crossed until the losses are acknowledged and the pain of the grief worked through. Finding constructive and healthy ways of expressing that pain and resolving its grip on the psyche of the congregation is necessary for the congregation to be freed from that grief to find adaptive and creative ways to embrace God's future.

In Conversation

To some extent, the pain of the loss of the past is present in many, if not most, congregations.

- Where did you recognize your congregation in some of the things you've been reading about and discussing in this chapter? Give specific examples.

- Discuss if and how sadness, despair, guilt, anger, the need to control, and a sense of anxiety and yearning are manifest in your congregation as you confront change and loss.

- How does your congregation respond in healthy and unhealthy ways to these grief reactions?

BIBLE STUDY: ISAIAH 40:6-11

Starting in Isaiah 40, we have the writings of the prophet known as "Second Isaiah," who prophesied in Babylon toward the end of the exile. His writings carry a mix of sadness and grief, hopefulness and God's promise for the future. Isaiah 40:6–11 is just one example of this prophet's keen sense of the response of grief in the face of loss.

1. Read: Isaiah 40:6–11

   • Where do you hear sadness and grief in this passage? Hope and God's promise for the future?

   • In the face of Judah's experience of change, loss, and grief, what, according to Isaiah, is unchanging and dependable?

2. Think about your congregation's experiences of loss and grief.

   • When does your congregation feel like withering grass and fading flowers to you?

   • How does God shepherd you through times of anxiety and fear in your congregation?

   • What can you point to in your congregation and declare, "Here is your God!" How is God already at work among you? How might God be calling you into the future?

6

A Well of Tears: Expressing Our Grief

I am weary with my moaning;
  every night I flood my bed with tears;
  I drench my couch with my weeping. (Ps 6:6)

The older woman was leaning against a low cabinet in the corner of the fellowship hall, sipping her coffee and surveying the small groups of people chatting around the half dozen round tables that almost filled the front half of the room. Her melancholy expression drew me toward her.

"Good morning, Gladys," I said, giving her a smile.

"Good morning, Pastor," she said with a sigh.

"By yourself this morning?" I inquired. On previous visits, she had always been at one of the tables with a group of friends.

"Yeah . . . ," she said, her voice trailing off. "I was just thinking . . ."

"About?"

"About how much things have changed around here. You

know? I was just remembering when we used to have twice the tables . . . and they were all filled."

"That's a sad thing," I said, reflecting on the obvious sadness in her voice.

Gladys nodded. "And we had a choir back then too. They sang once a month. I was the organist. . . ."

I didn't know Gladys had been the congregation's organist. Currently, they accompanied their worship services with prerecorded music played on a boom box. The organist's position had been cut from the budget several years earlier.

"Do you miss that?" I asked.

Her eyes teared up. "Yeah. I do. A lot. I think about it every Sunday."

We spent the next ten minutes talking about her grief at all the things she missed due to the ongoing decline of the congregation. She expressed her fear that the congregation would close before she could have her funeral at the church. Her fear wasn't just about losing a place to hold her funeral. Even more poignant was her fear of losing the community she had been a part of for a good portion of her adult life. A community that had cared for her, supported her, and given her life meaning. A community that she had always expected to outlive her.

When we finished our conversation, Gladys thanked me. "I've never talked to anyone about how much I miss the way things used to be. Maybe I didn't even realize it myself . . . until now."

NAMING GRIEF

A congregation can begin to more intentionally address the pain of the losses they have experienced by naming those losses and talking about them together. Therese Rando says that mourners can be helped to address the pain of loss if it is put into proper perspective in three ways.[1]

113

First, the pain associated with the loss needs to be seen as legitimate. Too often, we respond to the litany of lament congregations sing by dismissing or discounting the feelings of grief the members are feeling, even telling them to forget the past. These messages delegitimize the grief, burying it and causing it to come out in unhealthy ways. Blaming the congregation for the loss of families, youth, and children; empty pews; declining budgets; and deteriorating buildings simply piles shame on top of the grief. We need to say—out loud—that the pain we feel at losing the vitality we remember is real and can be intense, and the fear and anxiety it produces within the congregation is to be expected. Not long ago, I said as much to a congregation council where I was visiting and, with astonishment, a member said, "I never thought I'd hear a bishop say that!" Legitimizing what they were feeling changed the whole tone of the conversation.

Second, we need to normalize the feelings of pain and grief the congregation is experiencing. In my pastoral care of grieving individuals, mourners often asked me, "Am I going crazy? Is there something wrong with me?" They needed to be reassured again and again that what they were going through as they grieved was normal (if indeed it was). When I assure congregations that what they are going through as they face decline is normal and has been experienced by others, I usually get two responses. First, people are relieved and exclaim, "We thought we were the only ones!" even though at some level they knew better. Second, people are depressed and sad to find out that the decline they are experiencing is going on in many churches and denominations. Usually, though, they are grateful that others have traveled the same road ahead of them and they are not alone on the journey.

Finally, the experience of grief and pain needs to be put in context, which in this case means that mourners need to understand how the grief process works. This is especially important if the mourner's theology and values suggest that Christians should not feel the pain of grief when they experience a loss. As I have said, grief is the natural response to loss. How an individual works through (or avoids working through) grief determines whether it is healthy or unhealthy. Teaching bereaved people about the grief process helps them understand their pain is part of a healing process. Knowing at the outset that the intensity of grief will lessen over time is a relief to many. Understanding the process can help the bereaved person gain a sense of control that is healthier than the illusion of control that comes with attempts to avoid and swallow their grief. Similarly, within a congregational system, providing a context for what members are experiencing can help them understand their grief and, as a result, express it in healthier ways.

SHARING OUR GRIEF

As we legitimize, normalize, and contextualize grief for the congregation, we begin to create safe spaces in the community of faith where individuals can share their memories of the past and express and explore their grief together in healthy and life-giving ways. This sense of safety and security is essential in order to have meaningful, open conversations about the pain, sorrow, and sadness we are feeling due to the changes and losses we have experienced. Openly sharing our grief can help us build solidarity with one another and offset the loneliness that often comes with bereavement.[2] Strengthening cohesion through open and honest communication can ratchet down anxiety, temper reactive grief responses, and break down polarities as we consider and embrace God's future for our ministries.

At the beginning of part 2, we discussed the importance of telling the story of your congregation with the loss left in it and how we might understand the broader context in which those losses took place. Expressing our grief goes beyond just telling the story of loss. To work through our grief, we need to reflect on the meaning of that story for us and for the congregation and explore the feelings contained in the narrative. We need to consider ways to constructively share those feelings—especially hard feelings like guilt, anger, and shame—with one another in Christian love. We need to encourage open and honest dialogue about how the meaning of our story has shaped us in the past, informs us in the present, and can guide us as we think together about the future. Finally, we need to develop tools for improving our communication, using conflict and tension creatively and strengthening our connectedness to one another.

For an individual, sitting down and sharing our experiences of grief with a counselor, pastor, or even a close friend is an important part of the process of healing. By sharing our grief and talking about what we are feeling and thinking, we begin to take control of our own story, the meanings that narrative has for us, and how we understand ourselves in the face of loss. For a congregation, the opportunity to share feelings associated with loss is equally important, and we need to create opportunities for these conversations to happen.

Like the individual, a congregation needs to feel like they have control of their own narrative. In a congregation gripped by anxiety, it is easy for an individual or small group within the congregation to take control of the narrative. The pastor who told the people at St. James Church (see chapter 4) that there was nothing they could do about their situation is just one example of an individual taking over the congregation's narrative. Another example can be found in a group of highly anxious members who begin having "secret" meetings or who threaten to leave and take their money with them if they don't get their way. Providing an open, safe place to talk about where the congregation has been and where it is going, the losses it has faced, and the grief it is experiencing can prevent an individual or small group from taking control and allow other individuals and the congregation as a whole to express their grief.

CREATING SAFE SPACES AND PLACES

Creating a safe space for talking about our grief with others will allow everyone in the conversation the chance to share the full scope of positive, negative, intense, and often unfamiliar emotions in an atmosphere where those emotions can be accepted and heard. A safe place is one where those present can be themselves and express whatever they are feeling about the changes and losses they have experienced in the congregation. It needs to be a place where people can laugh or cry, scream or sit in silence together. A safe place is one where people are committed to listening care-fully, being compassionate and respectful toward one another, and recognizing those in the room as siblings created in the image of God. It is a place surrounded by prayer and the constant reminder that God is present.

In many of the congregations I have been associated with over the years, creating safe spaces and places where open and honest conversations can take place would be a tall order. In one declining congregation I worked with, we planned a daylong workshop to discuss the ongoing conflicts in the congregation and work on issues of communication. Only two members showed up. When people were asked why they chose not to come, many minimized the conflicts, dismissed them as ultimately unimportant to the life of the congregation, or tried to explain them away. Others expressed hopelessness about ever resolving the issues. Some were just out of town.

Another congregation I am familiar with never spoke about a pastor who had embezzled funds from them many years earlier except in hushed tones in shadowy corners or in the parking lot. Newer members, even those now in leadership, had never heard the story and didn't know what had happened. The unresolved grief from this situation haunted the congregation and its ability to trust its leaders for years. This intentional and unintentional "selective forgetting" allowed the congregation to avoid dealing with their grief over this significant breach of trust and prevented them from working through their pain. Their silence and unwillingness to deal with their past prevented them from embracing or even beginning to imagine a different future.

For many people, having a conversation about the reality of loss and the pain of grief in the congregation can be difficult. It's difficult to share the hard stuff. It means admitting failures and shortcomings. It means confessing shame, guilt, and fear. It means being honest about anger and frustration and hurt. It requires heavy doses of confession, repentance, and forgiveness.

Beginning this conversation in a large group meeting or weekend retreat is not a good way to start. In my experience, it is better to begin with smaller conversations, using the natural groupings already present in the congregation. Some of those groups might include women's and men's groups, governing boards or committees, Bible study groups, and other small-group gatherings.

I highly recommend that a trained facilitator guide these conversations. Having someone present who knows how to process the hard stuff, so people don't get defensive or hurt, can keep the conversation from becoming counterproductive. A facilitator can also help group members move beyond a discussion of primary losses to identify and explore secondary and symbolic losses. This person (or persons) can be from inside the congregation, but an outside facilitator trained in grief counseling or therapy, group process, mediation, or family systems can be very helpful, especially in a congregation that is stuck in their grief or highly conflicted about the changes they have experienced. Pastors from neighboring congregations (from your tradition or others) sometimes have this kind of training, as do professional counselors and therapists and leaders from your denomination.

In Conversation

- Are there currently opportunities in the life of your congregation for people to have open and honest conversations with one another? What are they? *No. We haven't opened that door.*

- How are those opportunities to talk and share structured and guided?

- If not, how might you create or expand these safe places and spaces for these conversations?

- Think about natural times when the congregation comes together for other things (e.g., a Bible study, around worship services, or an educational event) and times when you could intentionally structure small gatherings (e.g., a weekend retreat or a summer Christian education series).

FACILITATING CONVERSATIONS ABOUT LOSS

When I lead potentially difficult conversations, I always begin by rooting them in Scripture and surrounding them with prayer. Philippians 2:1–11 is a good place to start. In this text, Paul encourages the Philippian community to "be of the same mind, having the same love, being in full accord and of one mind" (2:2). Paul doesn't mean they should never disagree on anything or have different perspectives or opinions. He doesn't mean they all have to think exactly the same way or grieve the same way. The "same mind" Paul wants them to share is the mind of Christ, which he then describes by sharing a hymn that lifts up Christ's humility, servanthood, and self-giving (vv. 6–11). Paul is urging the Philippians to share the same kind of other-centered love that Jesus teaches in the upper room on the night before he dies, when he washes the disciples' feet and tells them, "Just as I have loved you, you also should love one another" (John 13:34).

The Psalms, and particularly the psalms of lament, can also provide resources for group reflection and study as you prepare to talk about your experience of grief and loss.[3] The lament psalms are both individual and corporate cries for God's mercy in the face of grief, anguish, despair, sickness, sorrow, and threat. The laments can sometimes sound harsh to modern ears, but in spite of the cultural differences between then and now, we can still hear their honest grappling with our common human yearning to understand suffering and their confident declaration of God's steadfast love in the face of the changes, challenges, and struggles of life. The lament psalms both call God to account and praise God's faithfulness. Starting a conversation about loss and grief with a song of lament can inspire us to emulate the psalmists' honesty, forthrightness, and confidence in God's presence as we lift up our own litanies of lament.

After a time with Scripture and in prayer, everyone should be given a few minutes by themselves to think, write, or draw about what they feel the congregation has lost over the years and how they feel about those losses. Give people time to quietly think and reflect. Discourage conversations during these quiet times. Let people dwell with their own thoughts. At this point, participants should just focus on the experience of loss. Concerns about the present and hopes for the future come later in the conversation. (We will take that up in parts 3 and 4.)

Following this reflection time, everyone should be given uninterrupted time to share their reflections. A larger group can be broken down into smaller groups of two or three for this time of sharing. No one should be forced to talk, but everyone who wants to talk should be given the chance before anyone talks a second time. While someone is talking, everyone else's job is to listen. That's it. Just listen. Listen actively and attentively. No comments. No arguments. No judging. No rebuttals. The only questions should be for clarification and to make sure you are hearing the speaker correctly. Sometimes people will stop in the middle of their reflections to gather their thoughts or deal with strong emotions. Encourage participants to tolerate these moments of silence. That can be a challenge, because silence makes many of us uncomfortable and we are tempted to fill in the gaps with words. As people share their thoughts, don't move to problem-solving too quickly. That's what Job's friends did in response to his grief, and their advice and admonishments weren't well received. Simply sit with one another in the reality of the losses you have named and the stories you have told. As people offer their thoughts, it is helpful for the facilitator or someone else to take notes (not a verbatim transcript of who said what, just a list of the main points that are raised). These notes can be consulted later to make sure none of the concerns, issues, or topics raised are forgotten.

Remember, not every loss named will necessarily be negative, and not everything about a negative loss is necessarily a bad thing. For example, some may not mourn the absence of children in worship, preferring a quieter setting for prayer. The absence of a pastor may open up possibilities for increased lay leadership. Empty classrooms may provide space for a new ministry that has been discussed but never acted on. Different people in the conversation may have very different perspectives on what constitutes a "loss" and the level and intensity of the grief it generates. That's why listening carefully is so important. Members of the group may need to dampen their own filters so they can be sure they understand what the other person is trying to communicate.[4]

The goal of these conversations is both to hear one

another's unique perspectives on and reaction to the losses the congregation has experienced and to foster a sense of solidarity around shared and perhaps universal feelings among the participants. Listening care-fully to one another strengthens cohesion, deepens relationships, and builds trust. As a shared story along with a shared sense of meaning emerges, it can give the congregation the courage to begin looking forward.

In Conversation

- How could you covenant with one another to make sure people can be honest and open with one another?
- What barriers would need to be overcome?

ACTING OUT OUR GRIEF

The small-group conversations we have been considering mostly focus on how our experiences of loss within the congregation make us feel. But as I have said, grief is more than just an emotional response to loss. Expressing grief through intentional action can allow people to express and process the physical, behavioral, and spiritual aspects of grief in healthy ways. Constructively acting out grief can also restore a sense of appropriate control and address the feelings of helplessness and hopelessness that often follow the experience of loss.

CONSTRUCTIVE ACTIONS

Taking positive action is an important response to grief because it helps us openly and honestly acknowledge the truth of our loss and release some of the emotional energy of our grief. For example, Mothers Against Drunk Driving (MADD) was started in 1980 when Candice Lightner began working to change laws in the state of California after her daughter Cari was killed by a drunk driver.[5] Others have set up scholarship funds, made memorial gifts, and started foundations as a way of expressing their grief.

In a similar way, a congregation can act out their sense of loss through constructive actions that express the emotions of their grief. For example, organizing a day to clean out things you will never use again might be the first step toward repurposing unused space. In one congregation I served, we had a meaningful time cleaning out a basement area that hadn't been used in years. As we went through layers of old boxes and broken equipment, and sifted through piles of old Sunday school materials and musty, moth-eaten costumes from Christmas pageants past, members told stories about the things they were finding. It was like an archaeological expedition! Explaining how an old filmstrip projector worked to some of the younger members was amusing for all of us. Finding a box full of old photographs brought tears to some of the elders in the group. Events like cleaning out an unused space can create chances for informal conversations about the past that are nonthreatening. They can give us permission to grieve.

MARKING IMPORTANT DAYS

Another way to act out grief is to intentionally mark important days and milestones. For families who have experienced a significant loss, the first year of anniversaries, birthdays, and holidays can be especially difficult. Cherished family traditions can be painful reminders that a loved one is absent. The empty chair at the holiday feast is a physical reminder of the emptiness in the souls of those who sit around the rest of the table. I recently got a birthday reminder on Facebook for a friend who had been dead for several years. I sat there and stared at the screen for a long time, trying to decide whether to ignore it or share a memory of the person. Instead, I wrote a personal note to the person's spouse.

The Kansas City Hospice website is a great resource for information on coping with terminal illness and the grief process.[6] Their resource on marking holidays in the year following a death suggests discussing holidays in advance, considering each person's needs, putting some activities on hold, and deciding what should be changed to make things more bearable. Celebrating memories by finding a way to honor those who are no longer there, making a gift or donation in honor of a loved one, lighting a candle, setting out a photo album, or sharing stories are constructive ways to acknowledge a loss together.[7]

In a congregation, anniversaries and holidays can also be both difficult and important times to share our grief at the loss of past traditions, practices, programs, and people. An aging congregation that has experienced decline may no longer be able to carry out many of the traditions and customs around Christmas or Easter like they once did. Annual festivals or other events may be more than can be managed by the few people left. The anniversaries of significant deaths in the congregation often go unnoticed. Like a family marking the first year of special days following the loss of a loved one, a congregation needs to be intentional about these special days. If the feelings of grief around these traditions, practices, and programs are left unspoken or unexpressed, they are likely to bubble over in bitterness, anger, and resentment as those who remember them and yearn to keep them going are unable to do so. Instead, leaders, working with those most invested in these events, should explore ways to honor past traditions, name the grief at their loss, and mark their importance in the life of the congregation. Only by doing this can a congregation begin to imagine new or renewed traditions without causing an identity crisis or culture shock or major conflict within the community of faith.

The recommendations from the Kansas City Hospice website can easily be adapted to fit a congregation. Celebrating memories through sharing photo albums, honoring those who have provided leadership, creating time to share stories of the past, or making a special gift or donation can help call out the grief we feel and help us begin to move beyond a tradition, practice, or program that is no longer possible because of changes in the congregation.

Vacation Bible School was one of the programs the people at St. James Church really missed. At one point, they had tried to offer a VBS program for the new families moving into their neighborhood, but no one showed up. Members weren't interested in trying it again. Instead, a creative interim pastor suggested doing an "Elder VBS" and inviting folks from the nearby assisted living center to join them. At first, there was a lot of resistance to the idea. How could the few members left pull off something like that? But little by little, the idea caught on.

They wound up holding the Elder VBS at the neighboring assisted living center instead of at the church, because it made figuring out how to transport the elders who lived there unnecessary. During the three-day VBS they did all the things they remembered were a part of VBS programs from their past. The group read Bible stories, sang songs, had snack time, did crafts, and played games together (adapting for the older age of the participants). But more important than that, they talked about how important those old VBS programs were for them and for their families. As they shared their stories, they shared their grief, their sadness, and their nostalgia for those lost days. They only did the program for a few years, but it stimulated a discussion about reaching out in new ways to the families in their neighborhood. Acting out their grief freed them to imagine a different future.

In Conversation

- As you think about your congregation's losses, how might you act out the grief you are experiencing?

- What constructive actions could you take or how could you mark significant days or reimagine ministries in your congregation to acknowledge the loss, honor the past, and give opportunity to express grief?

RITUALS

Rituals are another way of acting out grief in constructive, life-giving ways. Rituals provide concrete, structured ways to express the abstract, confusing disequilibrium caused by the disruption of loss and the reactions of grief. Rituals contain emotions and allow us to express them in a way that is less overpowering and overwhelming.[8] Even simple acts, such as standing together to sing a hymn, holding hands in prayer, or sharing sacraments can provide a safe outlet for anxiety and reinforce solidarity and cohesion within the community of faith. Group recitation of familiar texts like the Lord's Prayer or the Apostles' Creed can create a sense of unity and continuity with the past when a group recites them together.

Rituals of transition and rituals of continuity can facilitate the expression of grief for both individuals and congregations.[9] Rituals of transition are "rites of passage" that mark a change of status, identity, or life stage. Transitional rituals surround birth, graduations, adulthood, marriage, death, and other key moments in a person's life. Rituals of continuity maintain and confirm the stability of life at a given point. They include rituals of greeting and farewell (like shaking hands) and rituals that connect us to one another (like eating holiday meals together or sharing Holy Communion).[10] Within the community of faith, both kinds of ritual are well known and can be used to express our experiences of grief and loss.

Most congregations understand the power of ritual, because ritual stands at the center of life together. Whether they are formal or informal, structured or unstructured, contemporary or traditional, weekly worship rituals define the congregation in many or most members' minds. Even more significantly, for many people the weekly worship rituals define their relationship with God. That is one of the reasons making changes in worship is so fraught with resistance and conflict and why losses related to worship often generate the most intense grief reactions, especially for long-time members.

When it comes to our grief, our familiarity with ritual is a mixed blessing. On the one hand, communities of faith understand the power of ritual to communicate, support, and reflect deeply held beliefs, values, and principles. We understand how symbols and signs point beyond themselves, give concrete form to the transcendent, and make abstract ideas tangible. On the other hand, when most congregations think about decline it is participation in the weekly worship rituals that comes to mind first. Worship is usually the last regular activity left in many small congregations, and it is held onto tightly, even when it becomes difficult to provide adequate leadership.

With so much emotional and spiritual investment in worship and when it is the object of so much of our grief, how can our weekly rituals serve as an outlet for our grief? The answer is in the question. Because there is such emotional and spiritual investment and grief associated with worship, it is one of the key places where a congregation can talk about and express their experiences of loss in a structured way. Preaching, prayers, and the service itself can be used to express our feelings and name the community's anxiety about

127

the changes the congregation has experienced. It is in worship where we have the best opportunity to explore what the Scriptures have to say about loss, where we can sing the psalms of lament; offer our sadness and yearning up in prayer; hear the story of God's faithfulness through times of transition, change, and grief; and invite people to experience the support and encouragement of the gathered community of faith. Worship is a natural place for us to connect to our past, the long history of the church and all it has endured along the way. It is also a place where we can pray together for God's guidance and for the Holy Spirit to show us God's vision for the future. It is in the rituals of worship where hopelessness and despair are responded to with the hope of the resurrection and the promise of new life. Worship can give the people gathered the language to express their grief, while at the same time opening them to the possibilities of new life beyond their grief. Worship provides continuity and a sense of enduring identity and belonging that can sustain us as we do our grief work together.

In addition to worship, ritual can be used in other ways in the life of the congregation to express grief. Rituals of thanksgiving and gratitude can be used to mark the end of long-time programs and ministries. Much like a contemporary funeral is often thought of as a "celebration of life," these rituals can focus on celebrating, validating, and lifting up all the ways this ministry of the church blessed those who participated and the people who were served. These rituals should also acknowledge and express the grief that comes with the end of something that meant a lot to the people involved. To focus on the celebration without acknowledging the grief can drive the more difficult emotions underground, creating a barrier to the congregation's ability to look forward.

Most congregations do a good job of installing leaders, but few do anything to mark the end of that time of service. Rituals of thanksgiving and gratitude can also be used to mark these times of ending in the life of the congregation and the transition to new leadership. Again, sensitivity needs to be shown for the person ending their service. Even if the ending is welcome, some level of grief will almost certainly be present.

It would be good to conclude a formal discussion about the losses a congregation has experienced or a structured time for sharing our feelings of grief with a ritual that lifts those experiences and feelings up to God. The ritual of prayer should surround everything the congregation does or intends to do. As Paul says, "Rejoice always, pray without ceasing, give thanks in all circumstances; for this is the will of God in Christ Jesus for you" (1 Thess 5:16–18).

In Conversation

Think about how you might use ritual to express your feelings about the past.

- How might you remember and celebrate the people, events, programs, and activities that have marked the life of the congregation?
- How might you use rituals of transition and continuity both to express your identity and open yourself and your congregation to God's future?

A LITANY OF HOPE

Expressing our grief through storytelling and action can release us from the trap of yearning for a past that is gone and will not return. Freed from our yearning, we can consider God's future for us and for our congregations. The purpose of grief is not to sever all ties with the past or forget what has come before, but to give the past a new place in our hearts and minds, so it can inform our futures without controlling

129

them. Grief never truly ends. As we continue to remember the past, the pain of what we have lost will continue to go with us, but over time, the pain will become less intense, and our tears will begin to dry. Our grief will become more like background noise than a blaring siren consuming our whole consciousness.

As we work through our grief, our litany of lament can slowly become a litany of hope. This transition is gradual and not linear. Grief overlaps and intersects and doubles back on itself. Good days are intermixed with difficult days as optimism and depression dance together, and hopefulness trades places with despair. But over time, we will catch ourselves starting to look forward more than we look back and find that the past is becoming more a source of inspiration than something we long to re-create.

As we are freed from the limiting grip of grief, we will begin thinking about how to adapt to changes we know cannot be undone. The litany of hope is a song of possibility. It is the declaration of our trust that God is at work preparing a future for us, even if we cannot see it. The verses of our litany of hope ask how we can proclaim the gospel of Jesus Christ in new ways to the new realities in the world around us, and how we might adapt our ministry to the emerging needs in the communities we are called to accompany and serve. As we begin to look forward, the scrapbook of memories that tied us to the past can become a sourcebook of wisdom and core values that guides us into God's new future for our congregations.

BIBLE STUDY: PSALM 6

Psalm 6 is a lament psalm that cries out to God for healing and hope. It touches on the powerful emotions of grief and the pain of loss. (You'll need printed copies of the Psalm for this study.) Read and reflect on it as follows.

1. Have someone in your group read the psalm out loud, slowly, line by line. After reading, sit in silence with it for three to five minutes. After a time of reflection, circle or underline the parts of the psalm that resonate with you or that raise questions as you think about your own experiences of loss and grief.

2. Share your thoughts with the group.

3. Have someone else read the psalm out loud a second time. Listen for what the psalmist is asking from God. As you think about your experiences of loss and grief, what would you ask God? Write down your prayer.

4. Call the group together and pray your prayers with one another.

5. Have a third person read the psalm again. This time, listen for words of hopefulness and promise. As you think of your congregation, what makes you hopeful? Where do you see God's promises unfolding? Write down your thoughts.

6. Collect up your group's litany of hope by creating a list of the things each person wrote. Read the list together in a spirit of prayer.

PART III

Opening the Blinds: Adapting to Loss without Forgetting the Past

Do not be conformed to this world, but be transformed by the renewing of your minds, so that you may discern what is the will of God—what is good and acceptable and perfect. (Rom 12:2)

The church elders sat in the dark room looking up at the ceiling. At least, that's what they thought they were doing. It was too dark to really tell.

"It was a good lightbulb," one elder said, mournfully. All agreed.

"I remember when we used to have Bible studies in this room. Before the light went out," another reminisced.

"And council meetings," added a third.

"My daughter had confirmation classes here. But that was years ago," said a fourth.

"It really was a good lightbulb," the first elder repeated. All agreed.

"Perhaps we should get a new lightbulb," a new voice in the room suggested. Silence.

After a time, an elder said, "We tried that. But it didn't work."

Another added, "And we are out of lightbulbs."

A third said, "And, even if we did have one, there is no one who can change it. We're getting too old for ladders."

The fourth said, "I could ask my daughter, but she doesn't come here anymore."

A thoughtful silence filled the room.

"It really was a good lightbulb," the first elder said with heavy sadness, then added, "I just wish the light would come back." And all agreed.

After another long, awkward silence, there was a shuffling in the room. A chair moving. Footsteps across the tile floor. "Then maybe," the new voice said, "we should just open the blinds."

Sunlight.

This parable reflects the experience of a lot of congregations when they think about the past. As we have looked at the grief process, we have sat with these elders in the dark room and considered the burned-out lightbulbs in your congregation's life, those yearnings for the way things used to be. We have considered the powerlessness and hopelessness grief can bring to the community of faith and the physical, emotional, behavioral, and spiritual reactions that result. Now, as we consider William Worden's third task, "To adjust to the world without the deceased"[1] (or what we have lost), it is time for us to open the blinds and begin to consider how we engage the present and begin to think about the future of our mission and ministry.

In part 3, we will look at how, in the face of loss, we can adapt to the present realities in the world around us and how those adaptations can be informed and shaped by the past. By exploring the roots of our faith in Scripture and the ground of our relationship with God through prayer; considering the positive values, qualities, assets, and stories that shape our identity; and opening ourselves to the insights, wisdom, and strength of our past, we can begin the process of moving through our grief, being transformed by the power of the Spirit, and stepping into God's future for us and for our congregations.

An Old Story in a New Key: The Roots of Adaptive Change

And the Word became flesh and lived among us, and we have seen his glory, the glory as of a father's only son, full of grace and truth. (John 1:14)

The little group of Christmas carolers piled back into my minivan, blowing warmth into their cold hands. We had just finished our first stop of the night. It hadn't gone too well.

"Pastor, you started all the carols too low!" one of the carolers grumbled. The others in the group nodded as we pulled away from the curb.

It was true. I've never had perfect pitch and had just picked a note that felt comfortable for my bass-baritone range. "I'll try something higher next time," I promised.

Changing the carolers into bass-baritones wasn't an option. Their voices were what they were, and they were all higher pitched than mine. I had to adapt to them. To pick a new key. When I changed my approach, things went a lot better.

Jeremiah, in his letter to the first people exiled from Jerusalem to Babylon, encourages them to adapt to their new surroundings. He tells them to build houses, plant gardens, get married, and have children. He encourages them to make a life for themselves in this new situation (Jer 29:4–7). Embracing this new life didn't mean forgetting Jerusalem. But it did mean adapting to the new reality where they found themselves.

Huh!

To, exile?!

As bereaved persons come to terms with the fact that their deceased loved one is not coming back, that the lost job will not be restored, that the broken relationship will not be reconciled, or that the heirlooms destroyed by the storm will never be replaced, they slowly begin to adapt to the changed world around them.

In the same way, as your congregation comes to terms with the losses it has experienced and works through the grief associated with those losses, at some point leaders and members will begin looking for ways to adapt to the present reality. The purpose of the grief process is not to wallow in the sadness, yearning, and pain of our grief, but to get to the point where we can take up life again. For a congregation, this means finding new energy for mission and ministry, new directions for congregational life, and a deeper sense of God's call.

From the time of Freud, the goal of the grief process was understood to be severing our bonds with what we have lost, so we can invest emotional energy in new relationships. For a long time, congregations have been told they have to forget the past so they can move into the future. "The past is past," those of us who have counseled congregations have often said. "Let it go." But in more recent years, those of us who study grief and work with grieving people have come to understand that the grief process is not so much about letting go as about redefining our relationship with what we have lost. We do this by adapting to the changes and losses we have experienced within our congregations. We have learned, too, that while yearning for days gone by can trap us in the past, nostalgic thinking can be adaptive. We now know that we can move forward without forgetting where we have been. As we work through the emotional, behavioral, and spiritual responses of grief, we are freed to begin this adaptive work.

ADAPTIVE CHANGE

Adjusting to the changed reality that results from a significant loss cannot be accomplished with quick fixes or simple solutions. As we have seen, the death of a loved one is a problem we cannot fix. In spite of our yearning to have the person restored to us, at some point we need to come to terms with the fact that, in this life, death is irreversible, and the person who died is not coming back. Dusting the furniture may be the beginning of moving forward, but working through grief requires much deeper changes in how we view and interact with the world. Facing the challenges of a changed reality requires changing ourselves, the way we think about our world, and the way we function in that changed situation. It means adapting to the changed world we inhabit rather than fixing it.

According to David Kissane and Sidney Bloch, being adaptive in the face of a loss requires flexibility, open and clear communication, and a willingness to work through conflicts and disagreements. Ronald Heifetz and Marty Linsky, of Harvard's Kennedy School of Government and cofounders of Cambridge Leadership Associates, provide us with a deeper understanding of how organizations like congregations address these challenges. Heifetz and Linsky make a distinction between technical challenges and adaptive ones.[2] Each type of challenge requires a distinct approach to change. Technical change involves problem-solving methods based on the knowledge of experts and specialized skills. This approach to change is useful when problems are well defined, solutions are readily available, and the implementation process is clear.

Many years ago, I built a house. I coordinated the project and also did a lot of the work myself. I had never done anything like that before, so I bought video tapes and learned how to frame walls, finish drywall, install cabinets, and stain woodwork. I spoke with "experts" who advised me along the way. I hired plumbers and electricians to do the work I was not certified to do. As far as I know, the house is still standing. Building a house is a technical challenge that calls for technical approaches to problem-solving.

In Conversation

- Make a list of some of the challenges in the life of your congregation that have required technical fixes. Think of fairly well-defined problems for which clear and readily available solutions and processes are available.

- Take each item on the list and frame the problem you solved as a question. Examples:
    - How can we pay a pastor?
    - What activities will get youth and their families to come to our church?
    - How do we replace our HVAC system?

Unlike technical change, adaptive change requires new learning and emerges from the collaborative work of those addressing the challenge. Facing adaptive challenges requires changes in people's values, attitudes, or habits of behavior.[3] Adaptive changes are implemented through experimentation, trial and error, and creative imagination. We work on adaptive challenges by working *toward* a solution—trying stuff, learning what works and what doesn't, and then trying again. Adaptive approaches are called for when goals are murky, the road forward is not clear, those involved need to engage in new learning, and the outcomes of new steps are unpredictable.[4] In adaptive change the participants themselves are changed as they engage the situation. This is a critical point when we consider the adaptive work congregations need to do in the face of their losses. Grief work is not about changing the world around us to bring the past back, but about changing ourselves to adapt to the changed world in which we find ourselves.

Grief and loss are adaptive challenges that call for adaptive change. As we work through our grief, the question slowly changes from "how can I bring back the one I lost?" (a technical question) to "how do I go on in the face of this changed reality?" (an adaptive one). Adapting is about adjusting so we can live without the one we have lost. It's not about forgetting the person who died, but about finding new ways of relating to that person and all that person meant to us. It's about finding the courage to open the blinds on our loss, uncover the windows that have always been there, and let the sunlight shine into our lives in new ways.

Like individuals, congregations often attempt technical fixes to address the challenges of loss and change in their ministries. They add a "contemporary" worship service or run a new stewardship campaign or take out a bigger ad in the newspaper. These technical fixes often fail to produce the hoped-for results. By viewing the changes in the surrounding environment as technical problems that can be fixed, congregations often become disconnected from their contexts, disoriented by the murky road ahead, and resigned to the losses they are experiencing. As congregations unsuccessfully try one technical solution after another, they wind up working against themselves and promoting their own helplessness.[5] This helplessness and the anxiety it generates result in congregations being resistant to new insights and unwilling to cultivate new skills and experiment with new approaches to ministry.

When technical fixes fail to turn things around in a congregation, it is likely we are dealing with adaptive situations. Instead of trying to hold onto or re-create the past, we need to begin considering ways to carry out our ministry in the face of the new reality in which we find ourselves. When we begin to think adaptively, the questions change. We no longer ask, "How can we pay a pastor?" but, "How can we do ministry without one?" The question is not, "What activities will get youth and their families to come to our church?" but, "What does it mean to minister to young families in our community?" The question is not, "How do we replace our HVAC system?" but, "What role does a church building play in our ministry today?" See the difference?

In Conversation

Look at the list of technical problems and challenges you made earlier.

- How might some of these seemingly technical problems point toward adaptive challenges?
- Take each item on your list and rewrite the questions you are asking, so they lead to adaptive approaches rather than technical solutions.

As your congregation acknowledges and expresses the grief over your loss of the past, you will begin to see the futility of trying to address adaptive challenges with technical fixes. As you work through your grief, and begin to open the blinds and look at the world anew, you will come to a greater awareness of the changed circumstances in the world around you and begin to reshape your assumptions about that world.

142

These new insights will lead you to ask more adaptive questions about how to do ministry in new ways in your changed context.

But this adaptive work does not require us to ignore or forget the past, nor abandon everything that has brought the congregation to this point in your life together. Freed from yearning and a desire to re-create the past, nostalgic memories remind us how the congregation has adapted to changed realities in its past. We can then learn from those memories as we think about the adaptive work we need to do in the present. Nostalgia can help us develop a sense of continuity with our past, even as we move into God's future for our congregation. This nostalgic work begins as we return to the central stories of our relationship with God found in Scripture and the life of prayer that lies at the heart that relationship.

REROOTING IN SCRIPTURE AND PRAYER

The first time I met with my new campus ministry board, I listened patiently as reports were given. Decisions made at the previous board meeting were rehashed and then remade. Frustrations about a lack of student participation and an inadequate facility were batted around. The financial situation was agonized over, and there was lots of hand-wringing about how to turn things around.

After the meeting, which went on for three long, painful hours, the board president told me sadly, "They're always like this. Sometimes, if we really get into something, they're even longer."

I knew I wouldn't last long in this ministry if I had to endure these monthly meetings.

"Do you ever spend time in your meetings in Bible study and prayer?" I asked, already pretty sure what the answer would be.

"I read from the devotional book," she said, a hint of defensiveness in her voice. At the beginning of the meeting, she had read a brief reflection based on a single verse of Scripture. There was a one-line prayer at the end.

"No, I mean Bible study. You know, a significant block of time spent in the Word. Do you ever pray together for the students and the ministry, the campus, and the community?"

"We wouldn't have time for all that," she said firmly.

"Let's try it next month and see what happens."

At the next month's meeting, I started the meeting by leading a fifteen-minute Bible study and about five minutes of prayer. After we finished, the whole tone of the meeting changed. We finished our business in record time . . . two and a half hours. Over the next several months, the Bible studies and prayer time grew in length as the board meetings grew shorter. As our conversations about Scripture deepened and our prayer list broadened, our business discussions became more focused, creative, and productive. There was much less hand-wringing and much more adaptive thinking. The ministry itself began to change.

Since that time, I have continued to introduce extended periods of Bible study and prayer to the governing boards where I have served as pastor. In each case the effect has been similar. I have encouraged including time for Bible study and prayer in every committee and group, including committees like property and finance that aren't directly related to planning ministry programs and activities.

Rerooting a congregation in Scripture and prayer is the first, necessary step in adapting to the changed reality that comes with the loss of the past. Scripture and prayer must be foundational to everything else we do in a congregation, especially when we are facing adaptive challenges. The most important nostalgic memory in every Christian church should be the story of the life, death, and resurrection of Jesus and of God's mission to reconcile the world to God's self.

This memory has been the basis for the life of the church since the day Jesus invited his first disciples to leave their nets and follow him. Jesus's life of compassion, mercy, forgiveness, peace, and justice is the model for the church's life. Jesus's proclamation of the reign of God and his call to return to God's way should be central in defining who we are as the people of God. As we adapt our ministries to serve the world and proclaim the good news, we need to remember God goes with us, just as God has always gone with God's people. Looking at the changing world around us through the lens of Scripture can help us see that God is always inviting us to join the ministry God is already doing among our neighbors.

Pastor, attorney, and researcher Martha Grace Reese, in her book *Unbinding the Gospel*, suggests that congregations interested in developing "real life evangelism" in their ministry should begin with an extended period of prayer. In one example, she asks a congregation she is working with to pray for three months before they do anything else.[6] Wise advice. Prayer opens us up to the guidance of the Holy Spirit, who, Jesus says, "will teach you everything, and remind you of all that I have said to you" (John 14:26). Jesus promises that the Spirit will guide us, especially as we seek to adapt to a changing world. Prayer not only affects those we pray for but changes us as well. As we lift up the world in prayer, we begin to look at that world differently and see God at work all around us.

Prayer connects us to the Creator of the heavens, the earth, our congregation; it connects you and me to the root of life and the source of being. Prayer connects us to the meaning of meaning. It's hard to put this into words. Philosophers, poets, and mystics have tried for centuries. The bottom line is that our relationship with God in Christ lies deeper than our patterns and practices of ministry, and deeper than our congregation's identity and self-image.

Through our study of Scripture and practice of prayer, some of our assumptions about the church and the world will be affirmed, while other aspects may be challenged. Remembering all that God has done for God's people through the centuries and for us through Christ validates our assumptions that God is trustworthy and that the gospel is powerful good news for people. The story of Christ's death and resurrection affirms our belief that love is stronger than hate, forgiveness is stronger than judgment, gratitude is stronger than greed, and life is stronger than death. These affirmations can give us the courage to adapt to the changing world around us, even as we give thanks for the past we have lost.

Our study of the Word and our prayers may also challenge the congregation's priorities and force us to ask hard questions about programs, activities, and events we hold dear, including how we worship. One congregation where I served hosted a monthly fellowship event for several group homes in our area. The program consisted of a meal, entertainment, and opportunities for the residents to visit with each other. One year, following a Bible study about the inclusive nature of God's love, someone wondered if our monthly guests had ever been invited to worship. Sadly, the answer was no.

"I don't think they would enjoy our worship services," another person in the group said.

The person who asked the question said, "Maybe. But I think we should still invite them to Christmas Eve services next month."

One of the group homes accepted our invitation, and several of the residents became regular participants in our weekly worship as well. Their presence taught us a great deal and made us think in new ways about what it means to be a welcoming community.

As we adjust to the changed reality around us and begin

to think more adaptively about our ministry, many of our assumptions about the church and its place in society and the world are likely to be challenged. The assumptions that the church has a central place in American society, that our neighbors understand the basics of Christian theology and practice, and that belonging to a religious institution is a necessary and worthwhile part of being faithful are all being challenged by the changes in society that we discussed in chapter 4.

During one council Bible study, we were discussing some of our community service work when a council member stopped us and asked, "So, how is what we do as a church different than, say, what the Rotary does?" His question touched off an interesting conversation that challenged our assumptions about what we were doing and why we were doing it. How would you answer his question?

In Conversation

- How does your congregation root itself in Scripture and prayer?
- How might you expand the time you spend in the Word?
- How might you more faithfully pray for one another, your ministry, and your community?
- What is it that distinguishes churches from other community organizations?

The stories of our faith and the depth of our relationship with our Creator can guide us as we adjust our assumptions and the approach to ministry that flows from them. Nostalgic memories of the way those stories and our relationship with God in Christ have shaped and formed the community of faith in the past mitigate the effect of the perceived and actual threat of these changes. These stories can remind us what is at the core of our faith practices and help us see more clearly those things that are optional in our life together.

Seeing what is essential can free us to make adjustments to those things that are not. Rather than look for ways to bring the world into line with our assumptions, these memories can inspire us to adjust our ministry to the realities we face. In a world where fewer and fewer people are familiar with congregational life, it is unrealistic to expect newcomers to understand everything that goes on inside the church building. Even members may not understand the difference between being part of a church community and being a member of other kinds of organizations. Learning the stories of our faith through the study of Scripture and deepening our relationship with God through prayer, we will be better equipped to translate and interpret what we believe and how we practice our faith to those beyond our doors.

The study of Scripture and a life of prayer can remind us of who we are and whose we are, and in so doing help open the blinds so that we can see God at work in the world beyond the walls of grief and loss that can bind us. As we rediscover our identity in Christ, we are freed to consider how the Spirit has been at work in our past, discern how the Spirit is at work in our present, and perceive how the Spirit is leading us to sing God's story in a new key as we embrace God's future.

In Conversation

Respond to each of these questions from two perspectives. First, ask how you would answer this question with respect to someone outside of the congregation. Second, consider how you would answer from the perspective of someone who is already a part of the congregation.

- How might your approach to ministry need to be adjusted because congregations no longer hold a central place in people's lives or in the life of the community?

- How might you communicate the good news of the gospel to people who don't understand (or worse, misunderstand) words like *grace*, *salvation*, and *justification* and who don't know much more about Jesus than his name?

- How might our understanding of God's love inform how we reach out to people who are unlikely to seek out the church for spiritual care and who have no interest in "organized religion"?

- How might our understanding that God can and does work through those "outside" God's people (e.g., Cyrus in Isaiah 44, or the Syrophoenician woman in Mark 7) open us to learn from the neighbors outside our doors?

BIBLE STUDY: JOHN 1:1–18

1. Read John 1:1–18.

2. Discuss the following questions.

- From the beginning, the Word of God has been foundational to the faith of God's people. How does the Word "take flesh" in your congregation? Where do you see the light of the Word shining among you? (Be specific and concrete with your answers!)

- Why was it hard for people to accept the light of the world? Why is it hard for your community of faith to accept the Light in the midst of your darkness? How might our inability to adapt in the face of change and loss get in the way?

149

- John writes, "From his fullness we have all received, grace upon grace" (v. 16). Where do you see evidence of this grace in your congregation? How does this grace shape your self-understanding and self-image as a community of faith? How might this grace influence you more? (Again, be specific!)

8

Being Who We Are: Adaptive Change and Nostalgia

But you are a chosen race, a royal priesthood, a holy nation, God's own people. (1 Pet 2:9)

St. Thomas Church, at one point in its ministry, was the largest congregation from its denomination in the region. With well over a thousand members, the congregation had two pastors, full-time youth and music directors, and a large support staff. The three weekend worship services—two traditional and one contemporary—were always comfortably full, and visitors and newcomers were almost always present. The congregation was actively involved in the community, hosting the area food bank and supporting a homeless shelter and the local senior center. The youth group often needed two school buses to travel to off-site events, and the congregation frequently hosted community events for children and youth.

That was then. No one was exactly sure when the decline

started. Little by little, people started drifting away. The children grew up and left the community, their parents grew older, and no new families took their place. The slow decline was accelerated by a major conflict and frequent pastoral changes. At one point, a large percentage of the congregation left over a disagreement with their denomination's social teachings. A new megachurch was planted nearby and drew off the few remaining families with its active programs for children and youth.

By the time Pastor Johnson arrived at St. Thomas, the once-thriving congregation had declined to a few hundred members, and barely seventy-five worshipers attended the three services combined. The neighborhood around the congregation had changed dramatically, and most of the remaining members commuted in from the suburbs. No one in the congregation lived within five miles of the church. Conflict continued to divide the remaining members, and arguments frequently erupted in the entryway before and after worship services.

Pastor Johnson proved to be a healing, calming, light-hearted presence in the congregation, which helped lower the anxiety of the members. In one of his early sermons, he told the congregation, "You need to be who you are." He further explained that they needed to adjust their ministry to match the reality of who they had *become*. "We need to work together to figure out what it means to be a congregation of two hundred rather than a congregation of a thousand." With that invitation, Pastor Johnson started a process that slowly led to the transformation of the congregation from a conflicted, divided, and hurting community trapped in their grief, to a small, vibrant congregation that was learning new ways to connect to one another and to the community around them.

As we work to adapt to the losses we have experienced

(Worden's third task), we need to adjust our understanding of ourselves to account for our new reality. Loss changes us. As we work through the pain of our grief (Worden's second task), we slowly come to terms with those changes and what they mean for our lives going forward. To quote Pastor Johnson, we need to "be who we are," or rather we need to learn how to "be who we've become." However, being who we've become does not mean forgetting who we've been. Exploring our nostalgic memories and reconnecting with the best of who we have been in the past can give us strength and courage for stepping into the future.

LOSS CHANGES OUR SENSE OF SELF

Learning to "be who we are" begins shortly after experiencing a significant loss. Our sense of self is almost immediately affected as we struggle to cope with and then adapt to the effect loss has on our everyday functioning. New chores may need attending to. Finances may need to be rearranged. Children may need to be cared for in new ways. Each of these new tasks may lead us to think differently about ourselves and what we are capable of. For example, a man I knew who had never balanced a checkbook before his wife died was so proud of accomplishing this simple task that it empowered him to risk taking on other things he had never done before.

Some adjustments come a bit later and take more time. The death of a spouse, for example, can dramatically change long-established patterns, and adjusting may take a long time. One woman I knew had, for years, put the coffee on every afternoon and then sat at the kitchen table to watch down the lane for her husband to come home from work. After his death, she continued this practice for months before adjusting her afternoon pattern.

Following a significant loss, relationships begin to change too. In spite of the highly individualistic era in which we live, human beings are essentially social beings who need to belong. Because we were created for community, establishing and maintaining close personal bonds is critical for both psychological and physical health.[1] This fundamental need to be connected is often disrupted as relationships and patterns of life change following a significant loss. For example, people often treat survivors differently. They avoid "bringing up" the loss and, in doing so, isolate the bereaved person in their grief, leaving them feeling disconnected and alone. Friends sometimes stay away from the bereaved because they don't know what to say or are afraid they might say the wrong thing, causing the friendships to fall apart. As relationships change, and the social networks that previously supported us weaken, our self-esteem can suffer and our sense of self-worth can decline. Because our relationships and interpersonal bonds contribute to the way we understand our place in the world, these changes can leave us feeling out of place and damage our sense of continuity with the past and the present.

LOSS CHANGES CONGREGATIONS TOO

Loss can change relationships and roles within a congregation as well and have a similar impact on a congregation's identity—its sense of itself, its understanding of ministry, and what it means to be a community of faith. As a congregation declines or grows, personal and other relationships within the congregation can change. Individuals in a growing congregation may grieve the loss of the close, intimate relationships they had when the congregation was smaller. Individuals in declining congregations like St. Thomas may grieve the relationships lost as people move away, die, or leave the congregation for other reasons. As pastors come and go, their different personalities, priorities, and ways of doing things can reinforce or challenge a congregation's self-understanding. A congregation that can no longer afford a full-time pas-

154

tor or finds it necessary to lay off other staff may need to rely more on volunteers or look for partners outside the congregation. These changes will almost certainly change how a congregation thinks about what can and cannot be accomplished in its ministry. Failure to adjust to changing leadership roles can result in unrealistic expectations and unhealthy behaviors. In all these cases, the congregation needs to mourn the loss brought by changing relationships and roles, and adjust to the changes those losses bring.

St. Thomas provides a good example of how changing relationships and roles can change a congregation's identity. When the congregation was large and active, members thought of themselves as leaders in their community and denomination. Community and denominational leaders often visited the congregation, and a number of local business owners, government officials, and other "movers and shakers" were counted among their members. The members felt good about all they did in their community and welcomed the recognition it brought them.

As they declined, relationships changed. No longer were they looked to as leaders by others in their community. They could no longer afford pastors with experience and the potential for long tenures. As conflict increased, members left, including many of the community leaders who had once belonged. As a result, the congregation began to see themselves as lacking resources and felt forgotten, abandoned, and ignored by the community around them and by their own denomination. Members found themselves apologizing to visitors and potential pastors for what they had become.

Under Pastor Johnson's leadership, St. Thomas began to adjust to its new identity as a small congregation and to adopt new ways of doing ministry together. In a similar way, a congregation seeking to adapt to the changed role of the church in today's society will inevitably need to adjust its sense of self and its understanding of what it means to be a community of faith. These adjustments go deeper than just doing a few things differently. This adaptive work will require more than technical solutions, like offering a new program or updating worship practices. This is not about giving the same old congregation a new coat of paint. It can be more like a major renovation project that requires moving walls and rewiring and replumbing the whole building.[2] It will require us to think in new ways about our roles and relationships—and even our identity as the people of God.

IN SEARCH OF A NEW IDENTITY

Grace Church was founded in the early 1970s to minister to the large influx of retirees from its denomination who were moving south from the northern United States and Canada. It was one of a number of congregations popping up in the same area to serve retirees. At first, Grace was very successful in recruiting new members. The congregation grew quickly as new homes were built and filled with sixty- and seventy-something transplants from the north. Many of these new members came with extensive church experience and brought memories from a wide variety of congregations to the fledgling new church. These newly retired folks had energy, skills, and financial resources to support the congregation. Within just a few years, the members of Grace combined their resources to build a large, state-of-the-art church complex to house the growing congregation. The church was a beehive of activity centered on a vibrant worship life.

The congregation continued to flourish until the recession of 2008 slowed the southern migration of retirees to a trickle. Grace started to decline. As members grew older and younger retirees stopped moving into the community from the north, the energy to maintain the congregation's many activities dwindled as well. Giving faltered. The congregation's worship life changed too. Empty pews and scattered worshipers weakened hymn singing. Fewer and fewer people were willing to serve on the altar guild or as ushers, readers, and assisting ministers, and the few leaders who remained quickly burned out. Increasingly, the pastor led the service on Sunday mornings alone. When the pastor left, the congregation was able to afford only a leader with much less experience. A cloud of grief settled over the congregation as older members died and others moved back north to be with children and grandchildren.

As time went on, it became clear that the congregation's identity as a "retirement church" designed to receive and care for people from their own denomination was becoming harder and harder to maintain, but members had no idea how to redefine their ministry. The congregation's self-esteem suffered as its self-image shifted from a vibrant, active ministry to one just barely managing to survive. Increasingly, members felt helpless to do anything to reverse the decline they were experiencing. This lack of self-efficacy resulted in growing anxiety and a sense of paralysis.

Grace Church's story is not an unusual one. During the church's postwar boom years we discussed in chapter 4, many congregations were started to serve a particular group of people. In my own Lutheran denomination (and I would assume in other denominations as well), this practice dates back to the mid-1700s, when the first Lutheran immigrants came to the British colonies from Germany and Scandinavia. Lutheran churches were started where there were Lutherans who needed ministry. Wherever these immigrants settled, they started churches to provide their people spiritual care and nurture in a familiar language and a setting that reflected their European homelands. This practice was then adapted to the changing context of post–World War II America. Lutherans, intent on serving people who were already

Lutherans, located churches and ministries near military bases, colleges and universities, retirement communities, and, in one case I am aware of, near a car factory that had been relocated from the north. As suburban life flourished mid-century, Lutherans joined the movement from the central city to the suburbs. Urban congregations often followed their members, or people left the existing congregation behind to join a new one in their suburban community.

Today, the original reasons for planting many of these congregations are gone, and those few members who remain are left to struggle with who they are and what their ministry is supposed to be. Immigrants from Scandinavia and Germany quit coming. Military bases closed. The car factory moved further south. Retirees stopped coming. Congregations established to serve farm communities before the advent of the automobile, paved roads, large tractors, planters, and harvesters have declined with their rural towns. Disconnected from who they once were, grieving for their lost identity and role, and trapped by a sense of worthlessness and a loss of purpose, these congregations yearn for their reason for being to return. That yearning, in turn, prevents them from imagining a new identity with a new future for their community of faith.

In Conversation

- Why was your congregation started?
- Who started it?
- What motivated them?

Think about your congregation now.

- How does it reflect that original intent?
- How is it different?
- What would you say is the primary purpose of your congregation today?

SELF-CONTINUITY AND THE FUTURE

As both St. Thomas and Grace Churches struggled to find new identities in the face of the changing contexts of their ministries and the declines they experienced, they also yearned to maintain some connection with who they once were.

Maintaining a sense of self-continuity—the ability to perceive oneself as extending backward into the past and forward into the future[3]—while adjusting to the changed realities following a loss is a common challenge for bereaved individuals. A continuous, stable conception of oneself is an important human need and contributes to an individual's psychological health and well-being.[4] As we have seen, however, the changes in relationships that often come with loss can disrupt our sense of place in the world. Part of the work of grief is to reestablish the continuity of one's life story by redefining one's relationship with what has been lost. Adapting to a loss includes adjusting the story one tells about oneself and fitting the experience of loss into that narrative. Adjusting to the new role as a widow or widower does not require forgetting that one was once a husband or wife; it does require

159

coming to understand the continuity between the earlier role and the current one. A bereaved husband or wife can continue to carry with them memories of their role as a spouse in healthy and life-giving ways.

In the same way grieving individuals need to cultivate a sense of continuity as they work through the grief process, so does a congregation. As roles and relationships change within the life of a congregation, and with them, a congregation's sense of who they are, a congregation can come to feel disconnected from their past and question their identity. In the face of change, St. Thomas no longer saw itself as a community leader. Grace struggled to understand itself in new ways as the flow of retirees from the north declined. This shaken sense of identity can lead members to call into question the legitimacy of long-established ways of doing ministry. In more than one conversation about adapting to the changed reality facing a congregation, someone has said something like, "Are you saying we've been doing it wrong all these years?" These questions about the legitimacy of their past can cause a congregation to doubt the effectiveness of their ministry not only in the present but in the future as well, leaving them trapped and powerless to adapt to the challenges they face.

NOSTALGIC MEMORIES AND A NEW IDENTITY

The need to maintain a sense of self-continuity and forge a new identity resulted in tension in both St. Thomas and Grace as they began to adapt to their changed realities. Like these two congregations, most congregations are not willing to forget their past as they consider new ways of doing ministry. Exploring nostalgic memories can help navigate this tension as a new congregational identity emerges. As we saw in chapter 3, because nostalgia promotes social connectedness, nostalgic memories can contribute to a sense of continuity with the past and also inform the adjustments a congregation needs to make as it redefines its identity for the future.[5] Nostalgia does this by strengthening interpersonal bonds and fostering a deeper sense of belonging.[6] In the face of loss, nostalgic memories can also reinforce our sense of security and elevate our feelings of social support, keeping us from feeling isolated as we work through the emotions of our grief. In this way, nostalgia can contribute to the tasks of adjusting to the reality of loss and adapting to the changed world around us as a new identity emerges and we begin to consider doing ministry in new ways.

I saw this happen in a conversation I had with someone who was reminiscing about her experiences in a Bible study group she used to attend.

"I really miss that group," she said.

"What was it about the group that made it so special?" I asked.

She immediately zeroed in on the relationships she had with the people in the group. She told me how they listened to one another. Laughed together. Cared about one another. Felt connected to one another. They shared their lives outside of the group as well, attending family events and church, community, and school programs together. As it turned out, she didn't grieve the Bible study so much as the people involved in the study, though, no doubt, the group embodied the Christian values, principles, and theology they were studying together.

"Where do you find relationships like that today?" I asked.

She shrugged.

"Do you think people are still looking for those kind of relationships?"

She nodded. "They just find them in different places."

"What do you think that means for the congregation's ministry?" I asked.

Rather than talk about re-creating the Bible study group or dismissing the grief she was feeling, allowing her to explore her nostalgic memory opened up an adaptive conversation about making adjustments in the way relationships are formed and nurtured in the life of the congregation. As we talked about her past experiences, we started to think together about how people build and maintain relationships in today's world and how to create places where close interpersonal relationships similar to or maybe even completely different from the ones she enjoyed could be formed. We thought together about social media, coffee shops, pubs, gyms, and other places in the community where people gather, make connections, and encourage one another.

As we think nostalgically about how previous relationships in the congregation gave us meaning, we can discover new meanings in our current relationships and gain the confidence and openness we need for establishing new relationships. An experience I had can illustrate how this works.

Of the many people from the congregations and ministries I have served who have played a role in shaping my identity as a pastor and a person, Paul is one who almost immediately comes to mind. Paul died several years ago, and I think of him often. A significant leader in our congregation, Paul was deeply committed to caring for everyone and serving the community beyond the congregation. He had an amazing ability to bring people with diverse opinions and perspectives together, even as he was willing to share his own uncompromising position on political issues and congregational concerns. He could critique me without being critical, because I always knew he wanted to build me up, not tear me down. I miss Paul. I miss his honesty. I miss his faithfulness. I miss his example. I still carry him with me. I occasionally think about what he might say or how he might act in certain situations. I try to reflect some of his best qualities in the ministry that

I do. Like Paul, I look for what is good in peop!
cially new persons I meet.

For a congregation, sharing stories about fa
like Paul can give us insight and wisdom to d
think about adjusting to new realities and adapting our ministries to serve in a changing world. Paul knew the history
of our congregation and had a clear sense of our core values
as a community of faith, but he was also willing to explore
new ideas and try new things. He was willing to learn from
his mistakes and failures, and try again. His example, and the
examples of others like him, can inspire us to risk stepping
into a new future while staying true to the core of who we
are.

In Conversation

Think for a moment about someone in your congregation whom you knew
well, whose friendship you valued, and who is no longer with you. It
could be someone who has died or moved away.

- How did that person influence you, your faith, and your
  congregation?
- How did that person add meaning to your life?
- What might you learn from this person's example?
- Share these stories with one another. How do they reflect what
  is "best" about your congregation?

We all carry nostalgic memories from the congregations and
ministries where we have served and been members. All those
experiences can speak to our present life in the church. During my ministry, I have served in many congregations as a
called pastor, interim pastor, Sunday substitute, and workshop
leader. As a bishop, I am blessed to work with the congregations of the synod where I serve as they celebrate joys and
work through challenges. As I hope you can tell from the stories I've shared, I have learned something from all of them.

The nostalgic memories we carry often reflect times when we worked with others to successfully meet a challenge or times of shared joy and celebration that are meaningful to us. As we reflect on who we were in the past, these memories can be reassuring as we consider current challenges. Rather than delegitimizing the past, and our previous sense of self, nostalgic memories can reveal times in the past when we have successfully adapted to change and loss, and worked through and resolved struggles. They can remind us that we have been and still are loved and valued by God and by others—which is critical to maintaining a healthy sense of identity in the past, present, and future.[7]

As we mine nostalgic memories for the wisdom they contain, we are likely to become more optimistic about the possibility of establishing future relationships as our sense of social competence increases.[8] As we consider positive memories from the past, we come to believe we can have positive relationships and experiences in the future.

Even more significant, according to nostalgia researcher Clay Routledge, we are more likely to be motivated to pursue new relationships and experiences. Nostalgia has been shown to improve our sense of gratitude and our willingness to help others. Nostalgia increases our feelings of empathy and our willingness to donate time and money for those in need. It also leads us to be more proactive in resolving conflicts and disagreements with one another.[9]

Both St. Thomas and Grace congregations used nostalgia to maintain a sense of continuity with their past and learn from who they had been as their new self-understandings and identities began to emerge and they lived more and more into the congregations they were becoming

LEARNING FROM THE PAST

Nostalgic reflection can help us see that while much has been lost, the core of who the congregation is remains. Nostalgic memories affirm our continuity with the past even as a new sense of who we are emerges. Through nostalgia, we can discover and forge a continuing bond with the enduring aspects of the congregation's identity that continue to give the congregation life. Nostalgic memories promote growth as we remember how we have explored new ideas, taken risks, and tried new things in the past. The redemptive quality of nostalgia can help us reclaim times when we learned from failures and survived to celebrate success.

During his ministry with St. Thomas, Pastor Johnson helped the congregation rediscover its commitment to serving its neighborhood by reconnecting with that part of its past identity. While members couldn't re-create the broad range of social ministries they had been able to accomplish with over a thousand members, they drew on those memories to think about how they could honor that part of their story with a just few hundred people. Simple projects replaced complex programs. Rather than running their own ministries, they found programs to support in neighboring congregations. Building new relationships with other partners and organizations in the community opened up new doors for service and witness.

Grace Church's self-narrative, which reflected its understanding of its core identity, emphasized the importance of extending welcome and hospitality to newcomers, providing compassion and care to those in need, and fostering social connections for people who had moved a long way from their families in the north. Identifying these positive core values, drawn from nostalgic reflection on its past, began to open up creative new ideas about the congregation's current ministry. As they considered who among their neighbors might need welcome and hospitality, they began to think about how they could welcome the new Spanish-speaking immigrants coming into their community and how they might minister to and with them. As they considered who needed compassion and care, they were drawn to reach out to a local organization that combats human trafficking. As they thought about social connections, they reflected on the number of children who were regulars at the area food pantry where the members served and how members might become surrogate grandparents to the children.

Building on the foundation of our faith and the narrative of God's reconciling work in Christ, and drawing on nostalgic memories, congregations can discover the most life-giving, gospel-centered features of their identity. These positive core values and strengths give us the basis for adjusting our sense of self, adapting to the world around us, and exploring new ideas about mission and ministry. Through our nostalgic memories, we can come to a deeper appreciation of the strengths of our past for the sake of the future that God, even now, is preparing for us.

APPRECIATIVE INQUIRY

As St. Thomas and Grace Churches learned, identifying your positive core values and strengths and building on them is part of the work of adjusting to the changed reality your congregation faces. "Appreciative inquiry" is a change model developed in the business world and designed to identify the positive core in the narrative of an organization. It is a cooperative, coevolutionary search for the best in people, their organizations, and the world around them. It involves systematic discovery of what gives life to an organization or a community when it is most effective and most capable in economic, ecological, and human terms.[10] David Cooperrider and Diana Whitney, who created this model, have used it effectively to bring adaptive change to organizations as diverse as Roadway Express Trucking Company, British Airways, and the United States Navy. Appreciative inquiry has been used to foster change in congregations and other ministries as well.[11]

An organization's—and a congregation's—positive core can be discovered by exploring past achievements and innovations, positive emotions, organizational wisdom, core competencies, vital traditions, lived values, embedded knowledge, alliances and partnerships, relational resources, and a variety of other enduring characteristics and traits.[12] In a congregation, the positive core is made up of those things that have persisted in the life of the faith community, that make people feel good about being a part of the ministry, and that nurture their faith and spirits.

As described by Cooperrider and Whitney, the process of appreciative inquiry is composed of four Ds: discovery, dream, design, and destiny.[13] The first D, discovery, is the most pertinent to identifying the congregation's positive core and making the internal adjustments needed to think more adaptively about the congregation's ministry.[14] We will consider the other three Ds—dream, design, and destiny—in part 4.

ASKING APPRECIATIVE QUESTIONS

Using an interview process designed around "appreciative questions," discovery involves the whole community of faith in a conversation about the identity of the congregation. As in all adaptive processes, discovery is about learning together, collaborating with one another, and allowing new insights and wisdom to emerge from the conversations. Even designing the process is part of the process! The interview questions are all carefully shaped with an affirmative focus by a congregational leadership team that guides the process. Cooperrider and Whitney offer the following examples of appreciative questions:

- Describe a time in your organization that you consider a highpoint experience, a time when you were most engaged and felt alive and vibrant.

- Without being modest, tell me what it is that you most value about yourself, your work, and your organization.

- What are the core factors that give life to your organization when it is at its best?

- Imagine your organization ten years from now, when everything is just as you always wished it could be. What is different? How have you contributed to this dream organization?[15]

In Conversation

Take a moment to consider how you would answer Cooperrider and Whitney's questions. Interview another person using these questions. Report the responses to the group. Then, reflect on these questions:

- How do your responses reflect things that give life to your congregation?
- What patterns do you perceive in the responses of your group?
- How are the congregation's core values and self-understanding reflected?

In a full appreciative inquiry process, you would establish a team to develop questions and lead an interview process that would include as many members, friends, and other stakeholders in the congregation as possible. Following these interviews, the leadership team would analyze and map the congregation's positive core and identify themes and topics for further inquiry.

Unlike a deficit- or need-based approach to change, which dwells on problems to be solved and focuses on what has been lost or is lacking, the goal of appreciative inquiry is to investigate the past and present to identify enduring strengths and capitalize on assets for the sake of the future. Like nostalgia, which helps us to draw strength and confidence from past experiences, the purpose of appreciative inquiry is not to idolize the past, but to learn from it as you move forward in mission and ministry. For a congregation that is working through its grief and has started adapting to the changed environment where they are called to do ministry, this pivot from a focus on loss to an emphasis on strengths and assets is important to the resolution of grief and the taking up of new life.

Appreciative inquiry taps into the nostalgic memories of a congregation to articulate best practices, uncover unseen strengths and assets, and identify the best of what has been, what is, and what could be. Just as a bereaved person begins to venture out after the death of a loved one, the congregation that uses the process of appreciative inquiry can take the first steps in building new relationships and exploring new ways of being in ministry with one another and those beyond the church walls.

BE WHO YOU'VE BECOME

As your congregation adjusts to changing roles and relationships and begins to think more adaptively about responding to the challenges those changes present, you will begin to redefine the losses you have experienced and begin to learn from them. Over several years, St. Thomas began to appreciate the advantages, as well as the challenges, of being small. Grace Church started looking for newcomers in their community they hadn't seen before. Just as the people of Judah remembered God's promise, spoken by the prophets Isaiah

169

and Jeremiah, to preserve a remnant of the people after the Assyrian and Babylonian armies swept across their lands, the people of St. Thomas and Grace Churches started to find ways to draw meaning from their experience of decline and to see how God was at work throughout the process. As the blinds were opened and the light began to pour into the darkness of their life together, they discovered new relationships even as they reconnected to one another and drew strength from their past. As they considered new roles and began to think more creatively about how to do ministry, they came a long way in adapting to their changed reality; to being who they had become, not who they once were.

BIBLE STUDY: 1 PETER 2:9–10

1. In a few words, this short text lays out one of the best-known descriptions of who we are as God's people in Christ. Read through this "identity statement" slowly, letting each descriptor hang in the air for a moment:

> But you are a chosen race . . .
> A royal priesthood . . .
> A holy nation . . .
> God's own people . . .
> In order that you may proclaim the mighty acts
>   of him
> who called you out of darkness into his
>   marvelous light . . .
> Once you were not a people . . .
> But now you are God's people . . .
> Once you had not received mercy . . .
> But now you have received mercy.

2. Discuss the following questions.

- Which phrases resonated with you the most? Why? Which made you feel a little uncomfortable? Again, what made you feel that way?

- When you think about your congregation, which ones reflect your congregation's identity the most . . . in the past . . . in the present . . . in your hopes for the future?

- Where do you see concrete examples of these descriptors in your life and ministry?

A Place at the Table: Overcoming Challenges to Adaptive Change

Rejoice in hope, be patient in suffering, persevere in prayer. (Rom 12:12)

The people started gathering early, emerging from the dense, short trees of the bush into a large, grassy clearing in groups of twos and threes and fours. Elders, parents, children. A small group had formed by the time the pastor's mud-covered Land Rover pulled off the tire ruts that pretended to be a road and into the clearing. He removed a small table and folding chair from the back of the Land Rover, set them in the center of the group, and sat down, pulling out a ragged notebook bound with a rubber band.

For the next hour, the pastor jotted down the names of the people who would be baptized that day. An elderly man. A woman with three children. Whole families. Fifteen in all. A fairly typical Sunday. As the pastor took names and visited with these newcomers, the crowd continued to grow. A choir formed and sang a cappella songs as the people listened, swaying to the music and sometimes singing along.

When the registration was over, the pastor repurposed the table by covering it with a cloth, setting a cross at its center along with a small chalice and plate. The pastor pulled a graying white robe and a green stole from the back of his vehicle and dressed for worship. The choir finished the song it was singing, and a hush fell over the crowd.

"Grace and peace to you from God our Father and our Lord and Savior, Jesus the Christ," he said in Swahili, making the sign of the cross in the air. I recognized the familiar cadence, if not the actual words.

"And also with you," the congregation responded.

The open-air worship continued for almost two hours. Filled with music from at least three different choirs, a much longer sermon than I'm used to (or maybe it just seemed long because I didn't speak the language), fifteen baptisms, and Holy Communion, the time seemed to disappear. Even though I don't speak Swahili, and the music was African, and the outdoor setting of the service unfamiliar, the pattern of the liturgy I grew up with in Wisconsin was there.

The little table was again repurposed to hold the water cooler for the feast that followed worship. A Tanzanian "potluck" is a cornucopia of fresh fruits and vegetables, roasted goat, chicken, ugali (a stiff porridge made of ground maize), and plenty of delicious dishes I couldn't name. As in Jesus's feeding of the five thousand, everyone ate and was satisfied, and there were plenty of leftovers to take home.

This community of Lutheran Christians had adapted the ancient worship practices of the church to their Tanzanian culture and context. The worship proclaimed the gospel of Jesus Christ in a way that could be heard, and invited the people to participate in celebrating the love of God in a way they could easily join. I have worshiped with my brothers and sisters in Tanzania on multiple occasions and have been moved by the Spirit every time. Their Tanzanian way of doing Lutheran Christianity has helped me see my faith in new and powerful ways.

Humanity is a very adaptive species. Through the millennia, humans have learned to thrive in almost every climate and topography on the planet. From our beginnings on the steppes of Africa, we have learned to live in forests and mountains, cold northern climes and tropical rainforests, and even in the vacuum of space. The Christian church has proved adaptive as well. Transcending colonial attempts to force peoples into European molds, Christianity in the Global South has flourished, as it has adopted indigenous forms for worship, leadership, and other expressions of Christian faith and life. The Evangelical Lutheran Church in Tanzania is now larger than the Evangelical Lutheran Church in America and still growing. For the first time in one thousand years, the majority of Christians in the world do not live in Europe or North America. Today, one in four Christians lives in Africa.[1]

Adaptation to the changed realities we are experiencing in today's North American context is possible. However, thinking and acting adaptively can be challenging. Change is not easy for most of us. The grief that comes with change must be worked through along with other barriers that cause resistance and reticence to doing things differently in congregational life. In this chapter, we will explore some of the challenges we face as we seek to adapt to the changed realities we face.

CHALLENGES TO ADAPTIVE CHANGE

As adjustments are made in the life of the congregation and adaptations are explored, attempted, and reviewed, not everyone in the congregation will receive or accept them eagerly or even willingly. Resistance to change can be expressed openly or passively. Individuals can work to undermine adaptations, insist on clinging to the past, or simply refuse to participate in new ways of doing things. Adjustments made to address the primary losses experienced by the congregation can generate secondary losses that will also need to be grieved and worked through. For example, a congregation trying to make its worship more child friendly removed some pews to create a "children's area" at the back of the church. A family who sat in those pews stopped coming to worship because they felt they had lost "their spot" in the worship area. Another congregation reduced the number of committees to adjust to the smaller size of the congregation, and several longtime leaders felt disenfranchised when their positions were eliminated.

Let's be honest, adapting to a changed reality can be hard work for a community. Working through the complexity of this task in the grief process requires time, patience, and a large dose of (possibly unreciprocated) forgiveness, compassion, and mercy for one's brothers and sisters in the community of faith. Different groups and factions within a congregation may have very different ideas about what constitutes the congregation's identity. What you think of as part of the congregation's positive core may not appear positive to another member or group of members. Not all inquiries will be appreciated by everyone. In a congregation that has been severely divided by conflict, reconnecting to and building on past roles and relationships may not strengthen members' sense of community, but may instead dredge up painful and unresolved feelings about those who have left. Before the congregation can move forward, those painful and unresolved feelings will need to be addressed too.

GRIEVING DIFFERENTLY

In their book *Family Focused Grief Therapy*, David W. Kissane and Sidney Bloch address the issues of working with family members' different attitudes about and responses to the death of a family member and the grief work that follows.[2] Family members' responses to the death of a family member can be uneven. For example, I've seen families where one member's grief response is highly expressive with verbal sobbing, flowing tears, and animated gesticulations, while another member deals with their grief internally, preferring to sit quietly alone in their room, a blank expression on their face. The expressive member may think the quiet person "is not really grieving," and the quiet person may accuse the expressive member of being "melodramatic." This difference in grief styles can result in misunderstanding, resentment, and conflict. Temperament, personality, coping styles, and the relationship with the one who died can all affect individual responses to the loss. Family members may adopt a variety of attitudes toward a death, from callous indifference to self-recrimination. A family member who is self-absorbed will respond differently from one who has assumed the role and attitude of the family caretaker or peacemaker.

The variety of grief responses within the congregation can be even broader. As we discussed in chapter 4, the people who make up congregational systems come from a wider range of backgrounds and experiences than the members of most families, and the personality and history of the congregation can influence how people express their grief. Leaders need to be aware of these different responses, affirm that people can legitimately grieve in a variety of ways, and give people the space or the support they need to work through their grief.

TOLERANCE FOR CHANGE

Some families as a whole adapt quickly to changes, such as moving to a new community, taking different jobs, or attending unfamiliar schools. It is likely that a family with this kind of high tolerance for change will adopt new patterns in their family system more quickly than those with a lower tolerance for change. Similarly, within the congregation, people will have higher and lower tolerance for change and adaptive thinking. In my experience, people's ability to adapt to change follows a continuum. Roughly 10 percent of the people will quickly adapt to a changed situation, 10 percent will never embrace change, and those in between can go either way depending on the situation.

Before beginning the task of adapting to the changed reality faced by the congregation, it is important to "take the temperature" of the community of faith. If you have been working intentionally on the first two tasks in the grief process, you should already have a good sense of how the congregation is feeling and how the grief work is proceeding.

I wouldn't suggest pushing adaptive work too quickly. The congregation needs to be ready for adaptive work, or the conversations will not be productive or, worse, could lead to division and significant conflict. I've seen bereaved people pushed to adopt significant changes shortly after a loss that wind up compounding the person's grief. Usually these changes are not adaptive but technical solutions intended to solve the "problem" of grief. For example, a bereaved husband or wife is encouraged to move shortly after the death of their spouse. A young couple is urged to have another child after the loss of a baby. A divorced person quickly remarries or jumps into another relationship.

In a congregation, moving too quickly toward change can cause a congregation to shut down or rise up in protest. In one congregation, the new pastor suggested relocating the congregation within the first month after he arrived. The pastor didn't last long. In another, a quick change of worship times to attract younger members was met with petitions and secret meetings. Calling a mission developer to start a new congregation before the culture and needs of the community where the new church was to be located were understood resulted in a lot of money being spent with little to show for it.

CONSIDERING COHESION, COMMUNICATION, AND CONFLICT

Reviewing the congregation's cohesion, communication, and level of conflict is a good way to determine whether the congregation is ready to begin adaptive work. Kissane and Bloch suggest beginning every therapy session with a grieving family by checking these three key indicators of family functioning and health, because people's behavior can shift as the family experiences new challenges from their loss and as secondary losses arise.[3] Though I am not suggesting in any way that these conversations are "therapy," their advice is still sound. As you consider doing adaptive work, or even beginning a process of appreciative inquiry, it is good to check how the congregation is doing around these three key indicators of the congregation's functioning and health.

COHESION

- As you think about your congregation, can you identify examples of cohesion such as collaboration, teamwork, and mutual support? Think of a time when people worked together effectively or when the community came together around a tragedy, disaster, or challenge.
- As you have talked together up to this point, how have people responded to one another?
- Has there been tolerance for differences of opinion?
- Have people listened to one another?
- What got in the way?

Factions can divide a congregation, making adaptive work difficult or nearly impossible. Unwillingness to work toward consensus, attempts to control the conversation, and outright bullying can interfere with the new learning that can emerge from collaborative work. The other side of the coin can be problematic too. If the thinking of a congregation is too unified and the status quo is too entrenched, there may be an unwillingness to even consider experiments in adaptation.

As you do the adaptive work necessary for moving forward as a congregation, imagine ways that you can build relationships, encourage teamwork, and strengthen collaboration. There are plenty of websites that list simple team-building exercises to strengthen cohesion in a group.[4] Plan times of fellowship and gatherings to share and discuss ideas for adaptation. Use a process like appreciative inquiry to explore the past and think together about the present and future. Mix people up when doing small-group work or even during a fellowship time (though this has to be done carefully, as some people will resist getting out of their comfortable, familiar groups!).

COMMUNICATION

In Conversation

Good communication contributes to healthy cohesion within the community of faith.

Consider the barriers to open communication in your congregation.

- What gets in the way of honest, clear, and direct conversation?
- How are feelings expressed in constructive, healthy ways?
- How can our emotions become destructive within the life of the congregation?
- How are they avoided?

As we discussed in chapter 4, care-full, active listening is one of the cornerstones of good communication. As we address adaptive challenges in the life of the congregation, it is important that everyone has a seat at the table and that their voices are heard. As we consider our readiness for adaptive conversations, we need to ask, Who might be left out of this process? How can we make sure they are included? Homebound members and youth are often forgotten in these kinds of conversations. Inactive members are often left out.

Finding ways to listen to the community outside your walls is also critical to thinking more adaptively. When I facilitate these conversations in congregations, I often try to find someone from outside of the congregation to sit in and provide an outsider's perspective. In one such conversation, I invited the local Episcopal priest to join our Lutheran board as we were doing strategic planning.

"I don't know a lot about how Lutherans do things," she protested.

"That's the point," I responded. "Whenever we say something using 'in-language' or that doesn't make sense to you,

I want you to speak up. I want you to question our assumptions about how things are and how things should be."

She was a fantastic addition to our conversations, helping us see ourselves more clearly. She also helped us learn how to listen to one another more accurately.

One of the things I find valuable in the appreciative inquiry process is the way it encourages collaborative and inclusive communication throughout the whole organization. In appreciative inquiry everyone is invited to have a voice in the discovery of the congregation's positive core. This approach provides a broad understanding of the organization's strengths and ensures buy-in from the broadest number of people. By doing this, the decisions and plans that are made are more likely to succeed and the challenges easier to overcome.

CONFLICT

In Conversation

When there are conflicts or disagreements in your congregation, how do they . . .

- Help you learn from different perspectives?
- Get in the way of learning?
- Create division and contribute to factionalism within the congregation?

When do conflicts and disagreements . . .

- Allow different ideas and perspectives to rub up against one another?
- Lead to creativity and adaptive thinking?

Where do you see signs of tolerance, forgiveness, and reconciliation at work within the congregation?

As we have noted before, the absence of conflict in a congregational system can be as problematic as the presence of major conflict. As you make adaptive adjustments to the life of the congregation, conflicts are almost certain to arise. The question is not whether there is conflict, but how the congregation responds to and works through disagreements. Conflict can be a means of God's revelation of new directions for mission and ministry. For example, conflicts in the early church over the question of circumcision (see Acts 15) led to decisions that made it easier for gentiles to be included in the Christian community.

As you work through conflicts, it is important to search for common concerns beneath the presenting issues in the conflict. Work at getting everyone "on the same side of the table" to address these common concerns and to develop solutions together.[5] Always remember to listen! Inviting a trained mediator to help moderate the conversation can be very helpful. Think about how the congregation has successfully worked through conflict in the past, and consider what you might learn from those times when a conflict was not managed so well.

A cohesive community that communicates well also tends to handle conflict in healthy ways. That doesn't mean this work will be easy. But conflict in a cohesive community that communicates well is much less likely to cause irreparable damage to the community. In Matthew 18, Jesus presents us with a process for addressing conflict that involves, first, one-on-one negotiation; second, conversations mediated by a third party; and finally, arbitration by the whole community of faith. Jesus promises to be in the midst of our conversations and encourages his disciples to keep working at reconciliation. A cohesive community that communicates well separates people from problems; focuses on identifying concerns, not on defending positions; and works toward solutions that involve mutual gain for all those involved.[6] Congregations that manage conflict well anticipate, plan for, and design intentional processes to make major decisions, strengthen relationships within the congregation *before* conflicts arise, work to empower and encourage all sides in the conflict to express themselves and share their perspectives, and provide training in conflict transformation for their leaders.[7]

THE BEGINNING OF TRANSFORMATION

For bereaved individuals, "adjusting to the reality of the loss" (Worden's third task) involves adapting to life without the deceased loved one by redefining our relationship with the person who has died, shifting from a living relationship to one of memory. For a bereaved congregation that has experienced the effects of change, adjusting to the reality of the loss involves adapting to the changed contexts both inside and outside the congregation without forgetting the past. Working on the tasks of the grief process facilitates this adaptation and opens us up to new ways of life and ministry. Through grief, as painful and difficult as it can be, we are transformed and freed to embrace God's future.

As people of faith, we understand that this transformation is the work of the Holy Spirit who calls, gathers, enlightens, guides, and sustains us as God's people in the world. The apostle Paul calls on us as communities of faith to be transformed by the renewal of our minds and to use the myriad gifts God has given us for the sake of the gospel (Romans 12). By grounding ourselves spiritually, adjusting our sense of self, and redefining our relationships with one another and our past, we begin to experience congregational life in new ways. Nostalgic memories can inform us as we carry out this adaptive work and reimagine the future of our ministry. This transformative work can be the beginning of positive change, a new engagement in mission and ministry, and an experience of the new life that Jesus won for us on the cross. Within the congregation, we do this work together, bringing the variety of voices and perspectives within the community of faith and the larger community together at the table to draw strength and wisdom from our past and think creatively about our future. As Alan Roxburgh, a leader in thinking about the mission of the church in today's world, writes, "Transformation and innovation come not from programs presented by leaders but from the myriad ways ordinary people come to gather in dialogue."[8]

As we open the blinds to let the light shine into our congregations, we can come to appreciate in new ways where we have been and get a glimpse of where we might be going. As we look out the windows, we can see the world with new eyes. Instead of seeing a hostile environment that challenges our faith and threatens our existence as a congregation, we will begin to perceive a world filled with people who, like us, are yearning for light to illuminate the darkness of their lives, and who seek the very light that we know in and through Jesus Christ.

BIBLE STUDY: ROMANS 12

1. Read Romans 12 slowly, pausing after each phrase in verses 6–21 to reflect on how Paul's saying is evident in your own ministry and/or congregation. For example, after reading, "Let love be genuine; hate what is evil" (v. 9), reflect on how you express genuine love in your ministry. How do you stand against evil?

2. Discuss the following questions:

- Which phrases drew the quickest response from you? Which ones caused you to draw a blank? Why do you think that is?

184

- Where have you seen God's power to transform at work in your life, in the lives of others, or in your congregation? How is God at work right now renewing your mind(s)?

3. Reflect on this question: How are you and/or your congregation adapting to the changed reality in and around your congregation? Which of the following answers seems to fit your congregation best?

   a. We haven't started yet. We're still struggling with our grief.

   b. We're still looking for technical solutions to adaptive problems.

   c. We've started thinking about how to adapt.

   d. We have made many adjustments in the life of our congregation and are ready for real change.

   With your group, discuss why you selected the response you did. How might you move the congregation forward on this task? If you are reading on your own, reflect on what this response means to you and the congregation or community where you belong.

4. How can *you* personally become more adaptive in your own thinking about your ministry? What adjustments will you need to make in your spiritual life, your sense of self, and your relationship with others to make this happen? Share your thoughts with someone you trust and whose opinion you respect.

PART IV

Remembering Forward: Embracing God's Future with Boldness

Therefore every scribe who has been trained for the kingdom of heaven is like the master of a household who brings out of his treasure what is new and what is old. (Matt 13:52)

Max sat on a couch in the back corner of the coffee shop, staring down into his half cup of coffee. Strong. Black. Just the way he liked it. Some things would never change. But some things did. Sometimes in a big way.

He sighed. Two years. Almost two years since Sarah, his beloved wife of forty-five years, had passed away. Two years since she had been taken from him by the scourge that is cancer. Two years since she had . . . died. That word, *died*, was still hard for him. But a lot of other things had changed in the two years since she'd been gone. He'd changed.

The pain of losing her had subsided . . . for the most part. He still had days when he missed her terribly, but they were few and far between. He still thought about her most days, but it was different from how it was at the beginning. He remembered the good times and the struggles, but the intense yearning had dissipated. Now he felt almost like an observer to his own memories. Almost. At one point, he felt he would never be happy again. But these days, happiness seemed to find him. Well, most of the time. He felt like he was beginning to live again. That made him feel a little guilty at first, but now he felt free to take up life again without the pangs of guilt pulling at him from behind. He felt like he had got to a point where he could remember . . . and still move forward.

Max saw Henry come in the front door of the coffee shop and step up to the counter. Latte with a double shot of espresso. Henry was younger than Max, but it had been more than three years for him. Car accident. He had been a lifesaver for Max on some of the dark days. The whole little coffee group had been. He never would have dreamed that he'd become a "coffee shop regular." He'd never even been in a coffee shop before . . . before *it* happened. But that was then. Now, this little group of coffee-shop guys had become his best friends.

"Hey Max," Henry said, dropping into the easy chair opposite the couch. "Ready for your trip?"

Max was leaving for a ten-day trip to Europe in two days. "Yeah," he said, nonchalantly sipping his coffee. He was anything but. He was very nervous. It was his first overseas trip. He had never been interested in traveling before . . . before Sarah died. But traveling had become part of his healing. Part of the change. Part of the new person he had become. He had learned to be by himself. Learned to take care of himself. Learned to be himself. Sarah would have been proud. Puzzled. But proud.

Bill was the next to arrive. Decaf iced coffee with more cream than coffee. Even in the winter. Max often wondered, what was the point of that concoction? Bill's husband had been gone the longest. Over five years. Bill was Max's acquaintance from church and the one who invited him to join this little group. Max had resisted at first, but Bill had been persistent. Now he was grateful. Not only had Bill got him involved with the coffee group, but he had talked him into being an usher and invited him to join a Bible study. That was a lot for a devoted pew-sitter. Now Bill was trying to get him to run for church council, but that was more than Max was ready for. Maybe next year.

Two years. It seemed like an eternity and a moment. He was moving forward, and that was good, but Max also knew he would never forget. He knew, because that's just the way love works.

Based on my experience walking with grieving people, I believe Max's story is fairly typical. While the disruption of loss is the first and most dramatic change a bereaved person needs to face, the changes that come as one adjusts to the loss and begins to take up life again come more slowly over time. A small choice here. A little decision there. Making changes following a loss is often more like wading into the shallow end of the pool than doing a cannonball off the high dive. Sometimes those changes are so subtle they can be seen only in retrospect. But as time goes on and the grieving person adapts to the reality of their loss, a "new normal" begins to emerge. Larger, more significant changes begin to take place, new relationships are formed, new ways of living are embraced, and a renewed sense of energy and hopefulness about the future returns. As we live into these changes we blend the old and the new into a new way of being in the world.

In part 4, we are going to look at how change happens in a congregation as its grief begins to resolve and new ways of life and ministry begin to emerge. As we adapt to the changes that have come with loss, we are changed and begin to make changes that allow us to move forward and embrace God's future. As we begin this work, we are moving into the fourth task of the grief process, "taking up life again."

10

A New Journey: Taking Up Life Again

I pray that you may have the power to comprehend, with all the saints, what is the breadth and length and height and depth, and to know the love of Christ that surpasses knowledge, so that you may be filled with all the fullness of God. (Eph 3:18–19)

The task of taking up life again is "to find an enduring connection with the deceased in the midst of embarking on a new life."[1] Again, because William Worden's tasks of grieving are not "stages," we need to remember that these tasks overlap, interact, and intersect with one another throughout the grief process. The work of "resolving" grief in this fourth task emerges from the adaptations and adjustments of task 3 and learning how to cope with the emotions and other reactions to the loss worked through in task 2. This fourth and final task of the grief process does not necessarily mark the end of grief, but instead results in a transition into a new way of living in the light of the losses we have experienced. The memories of one's relationship with the deceased and the emotional connections contained in those memories continue for the remainder of a person's life.[2]

Max's story illustrates how, as the survivor of a loss begins to take up life again, they do not forget the one whom they lost or lose the memories and life-shaping influences of the years they spent with the person who died. For example, Max sensed Sarah would be happy about his decision to travel. He did not forget his relationship with her but instead understood that his life would continue to be shaped by the memory of the love they shared. Through the process of grief, the continuing bonds a survivor like Max has with the deceased finds an appropriate place in the survivor's heart and mind, so that they can live effectively in the world. Nostalgic memories of the life shared with the deceased inform the new person the survivor is becoming.[3] Though the deceased is no longer physically present, the abiding memory of the relationship continues to influence the survivor by providing inspiration, shaping values, and giving meaning to life even as new patterns of life emerge.

THE REALITY OF CHANGE

Someone (I don't remember who) once said that change is the only thing in life that doesn't change. It's true. Our lives are a constant process of change. Medical science tells us that we completely change our skin approximately every twenty-seven days.[4] The face we wear today is not the face we wore ten years ago or five years ago or even yesterday. The same could be said for the church. The church of today is not the church of a century ago or at the time of the Reformation or at the end of the first century CE.

The constancy of change is part of the very fabric of creation. In every part of the natural world around us, change is always occurring as either growth or decay. Even the great mountains with their majestic peaks are slowly changing as the elements wear them down. Silt slowly collects at the mouth of a river to form a delta, which gives birth to the unique ecosystem of wetlands and estuaries.

Each experience we have changes us a little. Some experiences change us a lot. Like all experiences, loss changes us. The only question is, How? As human beings with a certain level of self-determination and free will, we have some choice in how we answer that question. The fourth task of the grief process involves making those choices that lie within our purview and determining how, when, or even if we will take up life again. If we don't consciously engage this task, it is likely those choices will be made for us by others or by circumstance.

Change is never easy. Following the overwhelming change of a significant loss, the changes that enable us to take up life again are more likely to come incrementally—in slow, easily digestible bites. It took Max two years to get where he was in the opening story. Like Max, a congregation will require time, energy, patience, and commitment to embrace new skills and learn new ways of doing ministry.

Stony Creek Church was an open-country congregation in a wooded bend of a ravine carrying the small trickle of water that was its namesake. Surrounded by vast fields of corn and soybeans, the small, white clapboard church was located on a gravel road fifteen miles from the nearest town. Never large, the congregation was started by European immigrants who had come to the Stony Creek valley a century earlier. During its prime, farmhouses filled with large families dotted the landscape, and most of the members came to worship in wagons or on foot.

Things had changed a lot since those times. Most of the farmhouses were either gone or gray crumbling ruins. The children had left for the city, never to return. The land around the church now belonged to large family and commercial corporations that needed fewer and fewer laborers to work the land. A handful of older members still gathered at Stony Creek for worship each week and grieved not only the decline of their church, but of their whole community.

Pastor John had been ministering with Stony Creek for five years on a part-time basis. He had come to know and love the people of the congregation and its rural community. They knew of his affection for them and trusted him. They appreciated that he was willing to listen as they told stories from their past and recounted the changes in farm life and the church they had experienced over their lifetimes. He did not back away when they expressed sadness, frustration, and yearning for the way their congregation used to be. He was not afraid to talk about what would happen when the congregation could no longer sustain itself but also encouraged the congregation to keep doing ministry until that day came. He helped them discover and name their positive core and the strengths and assets they still had for doing ministry.

As he listened with patience and love, little by little the congregation began to believe that meaningful ministry was still possible, even if the long-term prospects for the congregation were limited. As the congregation began considering ways of adapting to their new context, they began talking about change. Some welcomed the idea of change. Some resisted. Others struggled. Everyone knew that, one way or the other, something different was needed.

Over coffee one Sunday morning, an old farmer and long-time member named Sam pointed out that the few remaining farm places near the church had a hard time getting internet access. Satellite internet was the only real option, and it was prohibitively expensive for many. After some conversation and using a small grant from their denomination, the congregation installed satellite internet and a few computers at the church and invited their neighbors to come and use them.

Sam and Carol went into the nearby city to attend a Saturday workshop on how to manage their fledgling internet café and develop a website. Unfortunately, only a few neighbors took the congregation up on their invitation.

Undaunted, the small group considered what they had learned from their experiment and then began imagining other ways to use their new technology to reach out to the nearby town, and that led them to look at other ways of connecting with people. They thought about trying to begin an in-town Bible study that would be linked through the internet to the weekly study held at the church, or hosting webinars and inviting the community. They looked for ways to get more involved in school activities and community events, including building a float for a local parade. They looked into sponsoring a youth soccer team in the city league.

In Conversation

Review the story of Stony Creek Church. Talk about how they did the following:

- Accepted the reality of their losses. (Task 1)
- Experienced and expressed the grief from losses. (Task 2)
- Adapted to their changing context. (Task 3)
- Began to take up life again. (Task 4)

How is their story similar to or different from your own experiences?

The fourth task of grief, taking up life again, is often the most difficult one for both individuals and congregations.[5] Individuals can feel like they are betraying the memory of a lost loved one by enjoying life again. Trying new ways of doing ministry in the congregation may feel like a rejection of the past and a devaluation of what has come before. But just as Max continued his relationship with Sarah as he established new patterns in his life, a congregation does not need to dissociate themselves from their past as they make the changes necessary to embrace God's future. Stony Creek was energized to risk reaching out to their neighbors in a new way because they could see the continuity between this new ministry and their founding principle—providing spiritual care to the people farming the land around the church.

Navigating the potential guilt and hesitancy of taking up life again requires balancing the need to work through our emotions and other reactions to the loss itself and taking concrete steps to adapt to the loss. As the grief process unfolds, the balance tends to shift toward adaptive work and toward discovering and embracing new patterns for daily life. Both of these tasks involve working through the changes loss inevitably brings and require us to make changes if we are to avoid getting stuck in our grief.

RESTORATION-ORIENTED GRIEF WORK

Researchers at Utrecht University, Margaret Stroebe and Henk Schut developed the "dual process" model for understanding the way individuals cope with the need to both address the losses they have experienced and make the changes required to take up life again. In this model, Stroebe and Schut identify two types of stressors that a bereaved person must confront as they grieve. "Loss-oriented stressors" focus on the deceased person and involve issues like separation distress caused by the physical absence of the deceased, struggling with the meaning of the loss, and redefining the relationship with the person who died in a world where that person is no longer physically present. "Restoration-oriented stressors" involve skill mastery, identity change, and other transitions and changes in the pattern of one's ongoing life and relationships.

In their research, Stroebe and Schut found that bereaved persons oscillate between these two dimensions of grief, working on one and then the other.[6] As grief work proceeds toward resolution, restoration-oriented work becomes the more predominant as loss-oriented work recedes, though it never disappears completely. As Max slowly stepped out of his grief and into new relationships, he learned more about himself and developed new skills and insights for living without his wife. He experienced changes in his own self-understanding as he went through a variety of transitions: from "married" to "widower," from one who had never been in a coffee shop to a coffee-shop regular, and from "pew sitter" to an active member of his church community. The dance between loss and restoration, grief and personal growth, continued as he both sensed himself moving forward and at the same time knew he would never forget his wife.

Congregational systems have similar oscillating experiences as they work through their grief at the loss of the past. In part 2 we focused primarily on loss-oriented stressors, including naming what has been lost, addressing our yearning for the past, and exploring the meaning of loss for the life of the congregation. In part 3, we shifted our focus to restoration-oriented stressors as we considered how a congregation adapts to the changed context for ministry. Here, we will look at how a congregation can be intentional about making the changes necessary to do ministry in new ways in the new contexts where we find ourselves.

Restoration-oriented grief work can be challenging. Like Max, a congregation that engages this restoration-oriented work may need to learn new skills, explore new places, build new relationships, and try new things as the congregation's identity and understanding of itself and its ministry changes. Like Stony Creek Church discovered, we need to engage this knowing that not every new idea we try will work. Knowing when we are ready to take up this restoration-oriented work and making the changes necessary to embrace the future is the central work of task 4.

In Conversation

Consider how Stony Creek addressed both loss-oriented and restoration-oriented stressors as they dealt with the changes in their farming community.

- Look back over your timeline and the losses you noted.
- Talk about how your congregation has worked through both loss-oriented and restoration-oriented stressors as you grieved those losses.
- Right now, would you say your focus is more on loss or restoration? Give some specific examples.

READY FOR CHANGE?

How do we know we are ready to take up life again? How do we know we are ready to embark on the new life God is calling us to embrace? Sometimes we are forced into making changes by circumstances beyond our control. But ultimately, no one from the outside can tell you when your congregation is "ready" to embark on a new way of doing ministry. But, though we cannot, from the outside, tell a congregation when it is time to take up life again, there are signs that the congregation may be ready to embrace change and the new life that is already ours in Christ.

RENEWED ENERGY FOR MINISTRY

Renewed energy for ministry is a good first sign that you are ready to embrace God's future and new ways of being the church. A couple of years after my first meeting with the demoralized remnant of St. James Church, which I described in chapter 4, a complete transformation had occurred. After two encouraging interims and the experience with their

Elder VBS, there was a palpable new energy in the small community of faith. They were beginning to dream again. Though still tentative about taking risks, they were willing to try some new things . . . within reason. A congregation ready to move forward will have a renewed sense of God's presence in their midst and of the Spirit's movement among them. As Psalm 121 proclaims with great hopefulness,

I lift up my eyes to the hills—
> from where will my help come?
My help comes from the Lord,
> who made heaven and earth. (vv. 1–2)

SEEING THE PAST AS A RESOURCE

Seeing the past as a resource is another sign that you have moved through your grief to the point of being ready to consider doing ministry in new ways. When a bereaved individual starts talking about a deceased loved one in the past tense, that is an early clue that the person is beginning to move toward taking up life again. Listen to how you and your congregation talk about the past. Are you still yearning to re-create the past, or has the past become a source of nostalgic wisdom that informs the present and provides encouragement for facing the future?

At Central Church, several of the members were talking about restarting their youth program. They designed a program that re-created the youth groups they remembered from their own teen years in the early 1960s, complete with board-game nights and guitar-led singalongs. They were perplexed when none of the youth from the congregation showed up. Several years later, they tried again. This time, instead of planning a program and inviting the youth to attend, they began by gathering the youth and their families together to talk about youth ministry. Instead of trying to re-create the past, they started the evening by talking about how the importance of youth ministry in their teen years had motivated them to restart the group.

After sharing their own stories, they asked the youth and their families, "What would make this ministry important for you?" They invited the youth and parents to reflect on that question together and to discuss what they hoped to see in the congregation's youth ministry. Ideas were shared and plans were made that were owned by everyone. It was a beginning of what, over time, became an active youth program that shared the positive core of the 1960s program but looked completely different.

READINESS TO BEING SURPRISED

Readiness to being surprised is the third sign your congregation may be ready to embrace God's future. The Holy Spirit has a wonderful tendency to do the unexpected. A congregation that is open to embarking on a new life of mission and ministry will be open to saying "Huh! Amazing! Never saw that coming!" from time to time. Maybe a lot!

Suburban Hope Church wasn't expecting that their partnership with an inner-city congregation would completely transform their ministry. But what started as a conversation with the city church about common concerns built bridges of understanding and friendship that changed the suburban congregation into an active ally and advocate for justice in the city. In another community, a campus ministry's weekly soup-and-sandwich program to raise money resulted in unexpected new relationships with faculty, students, staff, and local community members that built new partnerships and opened up new opportunities for ministry.

In Conversation

- How ready is your congregation to embark on a new life of mission and ministry?
- List specific examples of new energy, an ability to look to the past for wisdom, and an openness to surprise.
- What might you be willing to try, even without knowing the outcome?

LEARNING COMMUNITIES

In order to be ready to consider and implement change, congregations need to become learning communities. Because change is a constant, the work of learning about what is happening inside and beyond the walls of the congregation requires ongoing attention. Because of the speed of change in today's world, a congregation that is not committed to regular learning will quickly lose touch with its context and become increasingly ineffective in its ministry. Encouraged by Bill, Henry, and his other coffee-shop friends, Max was open to learning, growing, and trying new things as he worked through his grief, and it made a huge difference in his ability to embrace his new life. Congregations that see themselves as learning communities are open to exploring new ideas; putting things together in new ways; experimenting and learning from failures and successes; and finding teachers, guides, and partners who can instruct, encourage, and hold them accountable as they learn and grow. A congregation unwilling to explore old wisdom and learn new ideas dooms itself to decay. A congregation committed to learning opens itself up to growth and new life.

LEARNING COMMUNITIES ARE OPEN TO EXPLORING NEW IDEAS

Learning communities are filled with students, not experts. That is, they are filled with people eager to explore new ideas and learn new things. Students know they don't know everything and are always on the lookout to learn more. Every day is seen as an opportunity to discover something new. Students ask questions, are keen observers, seek out resources and wisdom, study what others have said and done, are open-minded and able to consider a range of possibilities, and integrate new knowledge into what they already know. By becoming students of the Scriptures, the traditions and history of their faith, the congregation's story, and the ever-changing community outside their doors, congregations can learn how these stories intersect with and inform one another, deepen their understanding of what they are already doing, and discover opportunities for doing ministry in new ways.

LEARNING COMMUNITIES ARE OPEN TO PUTTING THINGS TOGETHER IN NEW WAYS

Too often, we fall into the trap of thinking that being "creative" and "innovative" requires doing something completely new and different, something no one else has ever done before. Too often, congregations try to come up with the perfect program or formula for renewing life and vitality in their community of faith. But these attempts to discover and adopt the "next big thing" in ministry often fail. Fad ministries are about as effective as fad diets. Trust me, I've tried both.

The good news is that being creative and innovative does not require us to come up with something entirely new and different. Instead, creativity and innovation are more about putting old things together in new ways. They're about looking at what has been through new eyes and with new perspective. They're about rearranging the relationship of things and allowing something new to be born.[7] They're about bringing something old and something new out of your treasure for the sake of God's kingdom.

We've seen numerous examples of this throughout this book. St. James's Elder VBS would be one example. Central Church's youth program would be another. The Tanzanian congregation we met in chapter 9 drew together European liturgical traditions and Tanzanian musical practices to create a unique style of worship that fit their context. I've seen congregations explore ways to wed what they have learned from business, science, technology, psychology, and other fields to Christian understandings of mission and ministry in creative and innovative ways. Some of these attempts have worked, and some haven't. But all of them have helped these learning communities grow in their understanding of how to do ministry in today's world.

LEARNING COMMUNITIES ARE OPEN TO EXPERIMENT AND LEARN FROM FAILURES

Learning communities are willing to try something, fail, learn, and try again. Michael Michalko, a consultant and author who helps businesses and other organizations become more creative and innovative, tells the story of Thomas Edison's invention of the incandescent lightbulb in his book *Cracking Creativity*. Michalko writes that it took Edison nine thousand experiments to get the bulb to work. When asked by an assistant why he continued to persist trying after so many failures, Edison explained that he didn't understand the question. In his mind, he hadn't failed once, but had discovered thousands of things that didn't work.[8] In each experiment he changed a small thing until he achieved the results he imagined.

Within a congregation recovering from the loss of the past, as for any survivor of loss, taking up life again is composed of thousands of small steps moving toward the resolution of grief and the birth of new ministry. Congregations should start with small changes, make mistakes, learn from them, and try again. The urgency of loss can sometimes motivate us to make changes quickly and unreflectively, or prevent us from trying new things in the belief that failure will destroy us. But these anxiety-driven responses almost never move us forward. Slow, reflective, intentional changes that are attempted, evaluated, and learned from have a much greater chance of resulting in a working lightbulb.

LEARNING COMMUNITIES ARE OPEN TO FINDING TEACHERS, GUIDES, AND PARTNERS

To foster growth, learning communities—like learning individuals—look for teachers, coaches, mentors, partners, and guides who can instruct and encourage them as they take up new life. Max found Bill and his coffee-shop companions, who supported Max and cheered him on as he tried new things. Members of learning congregations read books and attend webinars, conferences, and educational events. They invite speakers to come in. They seek out other congregations and organizations to walk with them as they explore new ministry ideas. They seek out local leaders, business owners, and service providers in their communities to learn from them about the concerns, needs, and challenges they face and about the strengths, assets, and resources they have to offer.

I was with a congregation not long ago that lamented over the flourishing youth ministry program in a neighboring congregation. "They're not that different from us, but look at them now!" They moaned and spent the next few minutes hypothesizing about why their neighbor's youth ministry was so successful.

After a bit, I interrupted and asked, "Have you ever gone over there and asked them what they are doing that is working so well?"

They looked surprised and responded, "Why would we do that?"

Why wouldn't you? I wondered to myself.

Rather than seeing other congregations and ministries as competitors, being jealous of their successes and covetous of their results, wouldn't it be better to see them as partners on the journey? So far, I've never served in a community where there wasn't more ministry to be done than there were congregations to do it!

In my experience, collaborative efforts are more likely to build lasting change than individuals or congregations trying to go it alone. My friend Jonathan Strandjord, retired director for seminaries in the ELCA, once said that his definition of a good meeting is one where everyone walks out with an idea that no one had when they came in. I think he's right.[9] Change doesn't have to be lonely work. In fact, making adaptive changes is easier when it is done with others. We're just better together. Partners on the journey can help carry the emotional load of change; provide accountability, encouragement, and insight; give you someone to laugh with, cry with, and talk to; give you a much-needed outside perspective; and much more. Max would never have made the strides he did if it hadn't been for the friends who walked with him. In the area where I serve as bishop, we have been working to build small church and other networks with the idea that congregations will be stronger if they work together, share ideas and resources, and encourage one another. We restructured our synod into smaller clusters, so that now six to eight congregations can partner with one another in the geographic areas where they serve. In some places, it is already having a positive effect.

In Conversation

- How does your congregation learn together? List some examples.
- Brainstorm some new ways you might learn from Scripture, your past, and your community.
- What resources are available from your denomination? From your community?
- Where might you find partners to help you explore and implement new ways to do ministry?
- How might you discover what God is already up to in your community?
- Visit one or two congregations in your community and find out what they are doing.
- Sit down with local leaders, business owners, and service providers; listen to their stories; and use what you learn to inform your future ministry plans.

THE BREADTH AND LENGTH AND HEIGHT AND DEPTH

As individuals and congregations face their experiences of loss and work through their grief, the future can seem murky and uncertain, and the change uncontrollable and overwhelming. But as we become more ready to live into the changes we have experienced and grow in our desire to engage ministry in new ways, a new vision will begin to emerge. Making that vision a lasting reality in the life of the congregation will require us to identify first steps and overcome resistance but will also mean trusting the Holy Spirit to lead and guide us as we risk taking up life and ministry in new ways.

In Ephesians, Paul prays that the Spirit will help the young Christian community in Ephesus comprehend the breadth, length, height, and depth of what God has done for them through Christ and the love that is theirs because of God's gift of new life. By comprehending the scope and power of what God has done for us, Paul says, the community will be able to "accomplish abundantly far more than all we can ask or imagine" (3:20).

As we consider change and what it will mean for us to take up ministry in new ways in the life of our congregations, we too need to comprehend the scope and power of God's gift to us in Christ. Through this hope-filled promise, we can begin to imagine God's future for our congregations, and trust God to empower us to bring that vision to fruition in constructive, meaningful, and sustainable ways.

BIBLE STUDY: EPHESIANS 3:16–21

1. Read Ephesians 3:16–21 together, Paul's prayer for the community at Ephesus.

2. Discuss the following questions:

- What, specifically, is Paul asking God to do in this prayer? What effect will God's action have on the Ephesians?

- As you think about your congregation's readiness to implement changes and experiment with new ways of doing ministry, which of Paul's petitions is most urgent for your community of faith? Which have already been answered? (For example, you might need to be strengthened in your inner being but feel you are already deeply rooted and grounded in God's love.)

- Comprehension is about learning. How is God teaching your congregation about the scope and power of God's love for you? Share some examples with one another.

3. Conclude by reading the prayer again, this time substituting the word "we" for "I" wherever Paul writes, "I pray. . . ."

11

A Formula for Change: Stepping into God's Future

All of them were filled with the Holy Spirit and began to speak in other languages, as the Spirit gave them ability. (Acts 2:4)

The leaders of Redemption Church had known for some time that they needed to consolidate their Sunday worship services. The simpler eight o'clock "prayer service with Communion" had dwindled down to eight or ten worshipers, and the "traditional" eleven o'clock liturgical service was looking thinner too. There was little energy in either service, and the empty pews only underscored the decline the congregation had experienced. The council and new pastor were convinced the combined services would strengthen worship for everyone, and it would be easier for visitors and potential newcomers to participate if there was more of a community surrounding them. However, a council decision to consolidate worship services several years earlier had resulted in

protest petitions, members holding private meetings, significant conflict, and the eventual departure of the pastor.

Though the new pastor could see the need for the change,
she was wary of jumping into that fire too early in her tenure.
Convinced by the council that immediate change was necessary, though, Pastor Martha suggested beginning a series of
Sunday-morning adult studies on the theology and practice
of worship. As part of her study, she encouraged the class to
talk about their experience of worship at Redemption and in
other congregations they had attended. She asked how participating in worship services helped them praise God, dwell
in the word of Christ, express gratitude and thanksgiving,
and grow in their relationship with God. Many shared nostalgic memories of childhood worship services, holiday celebrations, and other special occasions. A few regular Sunday
worship services stood out in some people's minds. They discussed what they liked and didn't like about the worship
services they had participated in over the years. The class
mentioned the preaching, music, the choir, and the importance of receiving Communion. Then Pastor Martha invited
them to share their hopes, dreams, and wishes for worship in
their congregation going forward.

Following the adult study series, the council hosted several
cottage meetings in people's homes to talk about the worship
life of Redemption. Several people brought up the last, disas-
trous attempt at changing worship and wondered if that was
the "ulterior motive" of the studies and the meetings. The
council confirmed that making a change was a possibility but
assured those concerned that the whole congregation would
have a voice in whatever was decided. They asked how those
present would change the services if they could and received
many ideas—including comments from a few who said they
preferred things stay as they were, in spite of the poor attendance.

After the cottage meetings, the council published a report on what they had heard and invited the community of faith to spend a month of prayer and reflection on the future of the congregation's worship ministry. Prayer suggestions were printed in the newsletter and included in the prayers of intercession on Sunday morning. After the time of prayer concluded, the council proposed moving to a single, "blended" service at ten thirty with Sunday school for all ages preceding the service. The new service reflected the core worship values of the congregation that had emerged in the discussions during the adult classes, included practices that were unique to both of the previous services, and offered some innovations that were new to everyone. However, instead of just making the changes permanent from the start, they proposed trying the new schedule and other changes during the upcoming Lenten-Easter season. They promised to conduct feedback sessions toward the end of the Easter season to determine the future course of worship in the congregation and followed through on the promise. The congregation, with a few exceptions, agreed with the proposal.

By the time the feedback sessions were held in mid-May, several adjustments to the original plan had already been made and several more were suggested. While there were still a few detractors, most agreed that the change had been good for the congregation. After a lengthy discussion it was decided to continue the experiment for another six months. At the end of that period, and after further feedback, the change became permanent.

THE CHANGE FORMULA

Though they did not know it at the time, Reformation Church took an approach to change called the "Beckhard-Harris change formula," which has been used by businesses and other organizations for decades. I was first introduced to the change formula by my colleague Pastor Liz Albertson several years ago as we were discussing the need for change in many of the congregations in the part of the church where I serve as bishop. Many of these congregations knew they needed to change but didn't know how to go about implementing those changes without causing major conflict, division, and further decline. For congregations that want to make changes but do not know how to go about it, this formula is a wonderfully simple way to talk about implementing change. Since Pastor Liz shared it with me, we have used it many times to help the congregations we serve understand how to make change happen. The story of Redemption Church illustrates how the change formula, informed by the principles of appreciative inquiry, can result in a congregation embarking on a new way of life in their ministry without forgetting their past.

Developed in the early 1960s, the change formula has gone through a number of iterations over the years, but the basic premise of the formula has not changed. The most recent version of the formula is stated like this:

$D \times V \times F \times S > R$

D = Dissatisfaction or Desire

V = Vision

F = First Steps

S = Sustainability

R = Resistance to Change[1]

Surrounded by prayer and the study of Scripture and theology, fueled by the desire to change and a provocative vision, Redemption took the first steps together and adopted a plan for sustaining the changes. This process led to a new way of doing worship that both affirmed the congregation's long-standing traditions of worship and also embraced changes that breathed new life into their weekly gathering around Word and sacrament. Newcomers and visitors responded positively to the changes and several became regular participants in worship and Sunday school.

In this chapter we will look carefully at each variable on the left side of the formula, and then in chapter 12, we will consider resistance and look at some ways to overcome barriers to change.

D = DISSATISFACTION WITH THE STATUS QUO OR DESIRE TO CHANGE

The leaders and members of Reformation Church knew that change was needed. Dissatisfaction with the small number of worshipers scattered through the large sanctuary at the eight o'clock service made singing difficult and worship feel lonely. Thinning numbers at the eleven o'clock service made the liturgy feel empty and lifeless. Members at both services yearned for the church to be full again and to be surrounded by brothers and sisters in Christ as they worshiped and praised God, offered up their prayers, heard God's Word proclaimed, and shared the sacrament of the altar with one another.

The first variable in the Beckhard-Harris change formula is "D," for dissatisfaction or desire. For change to happen in the life of a congregation there needs to be some sense of dissatisfaction with the status quo or some desire for positive change. As we have seen, the disruption caused by the loss of the past can lead to both. However, even in situations where people know change is needed and even desirable, their yearning for the comforts of the past can outweigh the desire to change.

In a study we did in the Arkansas-Oklahoma Synod of the Evangelical Lutheran Church in America in 2011, we discovered what at the time was a puzzling paradox. While congregants expressed a clear awareness of the need for their congregations to change, they also clearly expressed their happiness with the way things were.[2] As we tested this finding in conversations with pastors and lay leaders, we discovered that, yes, people wanted change, but they wanted to change *backward* rather than moving forward. We learned that their happiness with the status quo reflected a desire to preserve the remnant of a past they had once found meaningful and enjoyable. For the survey respondents, the need for change they communicated was not about embarking on a new life but about yearning to re-create that lost past.

As we have seen, the desire to change forward emerges as a congregation works through the tasks of grief and comes to terms with the changes they have already experienced. Recent versions of the change formula focus on a positive "desire for change" rather than the negative "dissatisfaction with the status quo" as a necessary element for change to occur.[3] According to the framers of the contemporary version of the change formula, a positive desire to change is based on an appreciative understanding of the past that builds on strengths rather than deficits in the life of an organization.[4] This positive desire to change forward based on past strengths and values has the potential to bridge the paradoxical gap between an awareness that change is needed and a yearning for the way things used to be.

For Reformation, the level of dissatisfaction and desire expressed by the congregation council was enough to convince the new pastor that change was necessary. However, because of the resistance and conflicts caused by previous attempts to address concerns about the worship services, Pastor Martha wisely chose to move forward slowly. She knew that, by themselves, dissatisfaction and desire were not enough to make change happen. For real change to take place, the pastor understood that the congregation needed to see how any proposed changes could have a positive effect on

the life of the congregation without forgetting or abandon-
ing long-standing worship practices and traditions that many
held dear.

V = VISION

In the original framing of the change formula, the second
variable of the equation indicated that an organization needed
to have a "clear or understood desired state" in order to effectively implement changes. In other words, they needed to
know who or what they wanted to be as an organization.
Later formulations rephrased this variable as "a positive picture of the preferred future."[5] Having a vision for the future
is essential for a congregation to thrive. A congregation's
inability to see the possibility of a positive preferred future
will almost certainly lead to the decline and ultimately the
death of the congregation.

Coming to terms with the loss of the past clears the way for
envisioning the future. Developing an appreciative approach
to the past by reflecting on nostalgic memories allows the
congregation to draw on strengths, assets, and core values to
inform that emerging vision.

In chapter 8, I introduced appreciative inquiry, a narrative-
based process of positive change.[6] In that chapter, I said that
the first phase of appreciative inquiry is "discovery," which
involved identifying the strengths, values, and best practices
that make up an organization's "positive core." "Dream" is
the second phase of the appreciative inquiry process. Drawing on the positive core, the congregation involved in appreciative inquiry is invited to create a results-oriented vision
that answers the question, "What is the world calling us to
become?" Working collaboratively, the congregation envi-
sions its greatest potential for having an impact on their local
community and the wider world with the good news of
God's love and grace in Jesus Christ. As the congregation

215

listens carefully to their story, they share their dreams, hopes, and wishes for the future, which becomes the basis for this emerging vision.[7]

Following the interviews conducted during the "discovery" phase of appreciative inquiry, the "dream" phase begins by collating and sharing the interview data, and then working collaboratively to identify key themes for the congregation to explore further. This is not a matter of building a consensus but of drawing out compelling threads, linking them together, and identifying relationships and patterns in the life of the congregation that reflect times of excitement, creativity, and accomplishments.[8]

Though Pastor Martha at Reformation Church did not use the appreciative inquiry process, her decision to study the theology and practice of worship and invite members to reflect on their past participation in the worship life of the congregation shared many of the impulses of the appreciative inquiry process. Through study and nostalgic reflection, members discovered the positive core of their worship life and began to build a common vision for worship they could use to think creatively about the future of worship in the congregation. Bringing people together in cottage meetings allowed the whole congregation to be involved in the conversation about worship and work together to develop a new vision for worship that drew on the strengths and values of past practices and traditions.

Discovering a common vision for mission and ministry through an appreciative process is different from the common practice of developing mission statements to guide decision-making in a congregation. I used to spend a lot of time with the boards and councils where I served developing "mission statements." Each word in these short, carefully crafted statements was selected to carry a powerful message about the congregation's meaning and purpose. Too often, though, these statements were agonized over and then forgotten. I wonder, can you recite your congregation's mission statement, and, even more important, state how it shapes and directs your ministry decisions as a congregation? If you can, I applaud you. You are in a small minority.

A number of years ago, I gave up writing mission statements when I realized that the Bible gives us a number of clear, results-oriented, positive statements regarding the mission and ministry of the church. Why write a mission statement when the Bible gives us several to choose from? My favorite is the Great Commission, from Matthew 28:19–20, where Jesus says,

> Go therefore and make disciples of all nations, baptizing them in the name of the Father and of the Son and of the Holy Spirit, and teaching them to obey everything that I have commanded you. And remember, I am with you always, to the end of the age.

When I teach this text, I always follow up the reading by asking, "And what did Jesus command us to do?" The answer is, "He commanded us to love God, love one another, and love our neighbor as ourselves" (Matt 27:37; Mark 12:30; Luke 10:27; John 13:34). This command to love forms the positive core of the church of Jesus Christ and helps ground us as we shape a vision for what it means to love God, one another, and our neighbors in our contemporary context.

As we shape our vision for ministry, this command to love and invite others to follow in the way of Jesus is a necessary theme for us to include in our appreciative inquiries and as we mine our past for strengths, values, and best practices, and shape provocative proposals that draw us into the future. As we consider the past, a key question to ask is, "How have disciples been formed in this congregation, and how has our love for God, one another, and the neighbor been experienced and shared?" Answering this question will get us a long way toward discovering a congregation's positive core.

Several years ago, I was leading a strategic planning retreat for a small congregation that was interested in reaching out in new ways. I started the retreat by writing the word "church" on the top of a sheet of newsprint. Then I asked the small group to start naming words that described a church for them. They listed "family," "community," "fellowship," and a variety of other things. We filled the first sheet and moved on to the second. About halfway down the second sheet, I stopped the group and asked them what was missing. Nowhere had they mentioned "God" or "Jesus" or "faith" or even "worship." They blushed with embarrassment. Of course, those things were important to them! As we dream about our vision for what the church is called to be today, it is important that we remember to "keep the main thing the main thing."

In Conversation

- As you think about the story of your congregation, how has your love for God, one another, and your neighbor been embodied in your ministry in the past?

- How is it evident in what you are doing now?

- How might it shape your vision for mission and ministry in the future?

- What does it mean to "make disciples of all nations" today?

- How might you go about inviting others to participate in God's love for us and for the world?

F = FIRST STEPS

A well-known Chinese proverb says, "The journey of a thousand miles begins with a single step."[9] The wisdom of this ancient proverb is reflected in the third variable of the Beck-hard-Harris change formula, first steps. Having a vision is fine, but if it does not lead to concrete action, it is useless. A vision that is so complex it is overwhelming can be equally useless and prevent us from taking action. I have seen (and written myself) some vision statements and strategic plans that are so massive they become paralyzing. What a congregation needs to take that first step is something simple, concrete, and easy to accomplish that will build confidence and help the community believe that change is truly possible and desirable.

For Reformation Church that first step was calling for a time of prayer. Surrounding a change process in prayer anchors the discussions and decision-making in our relationship with God and opens us to the guidance and direction of the Holy Spirit.

While surrounding any decision in a congregation with prayer is always important, calling for a time of prayer does not always need to be the first step in implementing changes. I remember when we got our first "smart board" (an interactive whiteboard) in the synod office where I serve as bishop. Our wise treasurer at the time, who was a little skeptical about the new technology, urged us to get a "quick win" to demonstrate the technology's usefulness for our ministry with the synod. He was right. We needed that first step, and it took us a while to take it. Before we did, people were beginning to ask out loud why we had wasted all the money it cost. Skepticism about its usefulness grew. But once we took that first step—an electronic meeting with a couple of tech-savvy folks on one of our committees—more steps followed. Today, we regularly have meetings that use the smart board to electronically connect people separated by distance. We have used it for distance-learning classes and workshops, and for sharing resources and viewing media content during in-person meetings. It seemed like a huge change at first, but since we took that first uncertain step, it has become an indispensable tool for our ministry.

Someone (again, I don't remember who) once said, "Don't try to do everything. Just do something!" Max learned the value of that strategy when he risked accepting Bill's invitation to coffee. Carol, whom we met in chapter 1, finally dared to dust her son's room. Stony Creek Church subscribed to satellite internet. The folks from Hope Church got in their cars, drove downtown, and sat down to talk with their neighbors. Reformation tried a different approach to worship for a season. They all took first steps that opened them to God's future and the possibility of new life.

The third phase of appreciative inquiry is called "design." The design phase brings dreams into reality by creating "possibility propositions."[10] These propositions describe the congregation's ideal self, drawn from the hopes and wishes that shaped the vision during the "dream" phase. Possibility propositions push us to stretch beyond what we think is merely possible to imagine something that will challenge us and push us in new directions. These propositions give a congregation's vision concrete form and can be used to guide those important first steps.

Mark Lau Branson lays out five steps (not to be confused with the "first steps" we are discussing, but a way of getting to those first steps) for developing possibility propositions or what he calls "provocative proposals":

1. Focus on an area of the church's life and mission.

2. Locate peak examples (from the congregation's story).

3. Analyze factors that contributed to the faithfulness/ goodness of the church's life and mission in that specific area.

4. Extrapolate from the "best of what is/was" to envision "what might be."

5. Construct a proposition of what is possible, expressed as if it were already true.[11] (So, for example, instead of saying, "We will get to know the community around us better," a provocative proposal would say, "We know the community around us well and have significant relationships with our neighbors.")

In my experience, stating a provocative proposal as if it were already true and then working back from there to develop steps for implementing the proposal is a helpful exercise. As you take each step back, ask the question, "If this is what is going to be, what has to happen first?" So, for example, if your proposal is "We know the community around us well and have significant relationships with our neighbors," the step before it may be, "We have face-to-face conversations with our neighbors." Again, we ask, "If this is what is going to be, what has to happen first?" The answer may be, "We go out into the community and introduce ourselves to our neighbors." The process continues until you get to that all-important first step. At some point in this process, you will get to the question, "If this is what we are going to become, what is the very first thing we need to do right now?" Make sure that first step is something most people in the congregation have had input in shaping and can easily support, and in which they can readily participate, or no matter how provocative your proposal is, it won't happen.

In Conversation

Take one of your dreams for the future ministry of your congregation and begin working through Branson's steps for developing a provocative proposal.

- How will you get the whole congregation involved in shaping this proposal?

- After you have formulated this proposal, think about how you will implement that proposal by working back to the first step you need to take to make this proposal a reality.[12]

S = SUSTAINABILITY

Most of us have made New Year's resolutions to make changes in our lives that we have failed to keep. The usual pattern is that we maintain the changes for a week or two, then slip back into old habits. The diet we committed to disintegrates upon sight of the first chocolate chip cookie (speaking from personal experience). Similarly, as survivors of a loss begin to take up life again, their grief process can sometimes feel like one step forward and two steps back. A survivor's resolve to reengage life can dissolve as the pain of grief reasserts itself. Attempts at making changes in congregational life often fall to the same fate. I have seen congregations begin moving energetically down the path to renewal and revitalization, only to succumb to old patterns of unhealthy behavior. Nostalgic memories devolve into yearning. Failed experiments in new ministry result in a return to feelings of hopelessness and helplessness rather than leading to new learning.

In light of this human propensity for "Teflon Change," Steven Cady, associate professor of organizational effectiveness at Bowling Green University, and his colleagues recommended in the early 2000s adding "sustainability" as a fourth variable in the Beckhard-Harris change formula.[13] Without an intentional plan for accountability and support over time, even the best-designed plans will fail to take root and grow in the life of the congregation or individual.

In their process for family-focused grief therapy, David Kissane and Sidney Bloch recommend holding follow-up "consolidation" sessions with bereaved family systems after the conclusion of formal therapy. The first of these sessions takes place two to three months after the end of regular therapy sessions. During consolidation sessions, the therapist invites families to discuss areas that are still problematic or are hindering their continuing grief work and new family functioning. Following the first consolidation session, further follow-up sessions can be scheduled as needed to sustain the growth and healthy functioning of the family.[14]

As in these bereaved families, the progress of change within a congregational system needs to be monitored and the changes adjusted on a regular basis if they are to be sustainable. Reformation Church built in a process for adjusting their new worship schedule and for evaluating it after a trial period. Like Reformation, a congregation will better implement change if it identifies a time period to "beta test" a change rather than pursuing a plan until a train wreck results. During and after this trial period the whole congregation should be invited to give feedback. Following the trial, a decision can be made to either abandon the change, extend the beta-testing period, or adopt it as a permanent part of the congregation's life. At Reformation Church, the decision was made to extend the trial period after some uncertainty about the change was expressed, questions asked, and concerns raised. This decision to delay a final decision contributed to the congregation's ultimate support for a permanent change.

Participation by the whole congregation will result in greater ownership in the change and increase the chances that the proposed change will be accepted by the largest percentage of the congregation. On the other hand, involving the whole congregation in the evaluation process can also make it clear that it isn't the right time for this new idea to take root and grow.

I remember trying to introduce small-group ministry to one of the congregations I served. We had several meetings to introduce the idea and get feedback from the congregation that were fairly well attended. Before launching the new ministry, we communicated what the program was about and invited people to ask questions. There seemed to be good buy-in, and people seemed interested. However, when we launched the program, few participated. We barely got one group off the ground, and it only survived a couple of meetings. When we engaged the congregation in a discussion about why they chose not to participate, we quickly learned that, while most people liked the idea, they didn't have time to cram one more thing into their busy schedules. Learning from our experience, we tried again a few years later, only this time we integrated small-group practices into existing groups like the women's groups, the Wednesday adult study, and some committee meetings. That approach turned out to be much more effective and sustainable.

The final phase of the appreciative inquiry process is called "destiny." "Destiny" is about stepping into the future with a positive, affirming mindset that governs the way all decisions are made and implemented in the life of an organization. Because the whole organization is involved in shaping its future through the process of discovery, dreaming, and designing provocative proposals, David Cooperrider and Diana Whitney encourage "stepping back and letting the transformation emerge" as people engage the proposals at a variety of levels in the life of the organization.[15] In the congregations where Branson has introduced appreciative inquiry, he observed that innovations based on provocative proposals came from individuals, through pairs or small groups, from existing groups and organizations in the congregation, and through the formal governance structures of the congregation like the council, committees, and boards. Giving permission for members to self-organize, experiment, learn, and even fail created opportunities for new appreciative conversations to start in the congregation.[16]

Cooperrider and Whitney discovered that as the ability to think and act affirmatively became second nature in the organizations using appreciative inquiry (in contrast to focusing on problems and deficits as their default way of thinking about change), the more likely it was that the emerging dreams and designs became sustainable parts of the organization, and the more innovative and creative ideas emerged from ongoing appreciative conversations.[17] Within the appreciative inquiry process, accountability and support result from ongoing appreciative conversations to identify and build on strengths, shared learning from experiments, and a willingness to give people permission to try new things. Building in ongoing opportunities to reflect appreciatively about new ministries and make adjustments or let go of them in whole or in part will not only contribute to the sustainability of those ministries but also keep them from becoming ineffective fixtures in the life of the congregation.

Reformation's process for adapting to the declining attendance in their worship services resulted in sustainable change because they listened to one another's dissatisfaction with what was, explored their desire for what could be, worked together to develop a vision for the future of their ministry through study and appreciative conversations about their past, identified clear first steps, and created an ongoing plan for sustaining those changes and adjusting them as necessary. The new way of worshiping together that they adopted not only strengthened the worshipers' experience of participating in worship but also opened them to thinking in a different way about their ministry and God's future for their congregation.

In Conversation

Reread Redemption's story and reflect on your own congregation's ministry.

- What changes do you think need to be made in your congregation's ministry?
- Take that perceived need and run it through the change formula.
- How might you invite your congregation to collaborate on developing an adaptive change plan around this issue?
- How could your congregation give its members permission to experiment with doing ministry in new ways?
- How would you support them in these efforts?

HS = THE HOLY SPIRIT

As Pastor Albertson and I have discussed our use of the Beckhard-Harris change formula in congregations, she has suggested adding the power and presence of the Holy Spirit as a fifth variable. This addition to the formula is particularly relevant in a church that believes Jesus's promise that the Holy Spirit will "guide you into all the truth" (John 16:13) and will "teach you everything, and remind you of all that I have said to you" (John 14:26). Her adaptation would make the formula read:

$$(D \times V \times F \times S) \, HS > R$$

You will notice that the variables in the change formula are multiplied, not added together. This is significant in two ways. First, the various components of the formula have a multiplying effect. One supports and drives the other. The second is something we learned in elementary-school math class: if any variable in a multiplication problem is zero, then the product is always zero. If any part of the formula is missing, change won't happen.

At Pentecost, it was the power of the Holy Spirit that drove the disciples out of the upper room in Jerusalem and into the streets to proclaim the good news in languages the people could understand. In the same way, the Spirit can propel a congregation to speak the gospel in new ways to the people in our worship assemblies and outside our doors. The Spirit can multiply our efforts at change and help us to overcome the resistance to positive change that inevitably arises when changes are proposed.

As people of faith, we agree that all things are possible with God and that no good thing is possible apart from God. As we said in chapter 7, surrounding the process of grief with the study of Scripture and prayer is critical to healthy grief work in a congregation. As we work on the fourth task of this process, it is God's new life that we hope to step into as we move forward, and it is God's future for our congregation we intend to discern as we consider adjustments, adaptations, and changes to the way we do ministry together. Participating in God's mission and ministry should be the goal as we take up life again and embrace God's future as the people of God.

BIBLE STUDY: ACTS 2:1–13

Pentecost marks the beginning of the postresurrection mission of the church to bear witness to the good news of Christ's life, death, and resurrection "to the ends of the earth" (Acts 1:8). On Pentecost day, the Holy Spirit "lit a fire" in the disciples and drove them out of their upper room into the wider world and, as promised, gave them the words they needed to proclaim the good news. Through the Spirit, the disciples took up this new life of witness, drawing on all Jesus had taught them during their time together.

1. Read Acts 2:1–13. As you read through the story of Pentecost, think about your own congregation's journey through the grief process. Through these pages, you have worked through your experience of loss, explored the emotions and other reactions of grief, and considered ways to adapt to the changed contexts in which you are called to do ministry.

2. Now, in light of all you have discussed and learned, consider these questions:

- How is the Spirit lighting a fire in you and your congregation?

- Where is the Spirit driving you and your congregation in mission?

- How is the Spirit teaching you a new language and equipping you for this task?

- Is anyone accusing you of being "filled with new wine"? If so, how might you respond? (That's the subject of our next chapter.)

A New Creation: Embracing God's Future

So if anyone is in Christ, there is a new creation: everything old
has passed away; see, everything has become new! (2 Cor 5:17)

"I'd rather see this church close than change!" the man at the
congregational meeting said emphatically, pounding his fist
on the table and making the paper plates from the potluck
jump.

I had been working with the leaders of the congregation
for several months to develop a plan to turn around the
decline the congregation was experiencing, and the leaders
were presenting some ideas for the input of the members.

No one in the room disagreed. No one stood to challenge
his opinion. Even the leaders stood silent with furrowed
brows.

Finally, after what seemed like an eternal silence, I spoke
up. "Is that how everyone feels?" I asked my question tenta-
tively, afraid of what the answer might be.

Another man stood up. "Do we have much choice? I mean, I don't think any of those ideas will work. I don't think we have enough people to do all that."

A woman from the back said, "And we'd have to give up so much, it wouldn't be the same church if we changed the way we worship."

Another woman said, "How are we going to pay for it all?"

Another man said, "And is what you're proposing even Lutheran?"

No one spoke in favor of the proposed changes. The leaders felt demoralized. A few months later, the congregation closed.

Unless resistance is acknowledged and responded to, the chance of lasting change happening in a congregation is slim. While the leaders of this congregation thought they were in touch with what people were thinking and feeling, they underestimated the level of resistance to the proposals they brought to the congregational meeting. Surprised by what they heard, they lost energy, enthusiasm, and the will to lead the congregation forward in mission and ministry. Several of them resigned, and no one stepped up to take their place.

Up to this point, we have been focusing our attention solely on the left side of the change formula. However, if a congregation wants to embrace God's future, we cannot ignore the R on the right side of the equation: "Resistance." If we want real, lasting change to happen in the life of our congregations, we need to take resistance seriously and sincerely respond to the concerns of those who are resisting.

The Beckhard-Harris change formula is premised on the belief that if the multiplied effect of the change variables on the left side of the equation is not greater than the organization's resistance to change, change will not happen. Ensuring that the product of the formula leans toward the acceptance and sustainable implementation of change will require either making the case for change compelling enough to outweigh the resistance or reducing the level of resistance, so it cannot prevent the needed change from taking place.

In chapter 9, we discussed ways to address challenges to adaptive work in the congregation. We saw how cohesion and communication can be strengthened and conflict addressed in order to ready the congregation for adaptive changes. We acknowledged that people's personality, temperament, and own stories can get in the way of embracing adaptive thinking and acting. In spite of our best efforts to prepare the ground for change, resistance is inevitable and sometimes appropriate. Not all change is good. Not all ideas are worth trying. Sometimes the congregation is not ready, and an idea just needs to wait for another time. Sometimes important details are missing and our plans are incomplete, so we need to slow down to fill in the gaps.

Resistance is sometimes rooted in the obstructionist grumbling of the congregational curmudgeons, but it is often a symptom that concerns surrounding the proposed change haven't been fully addressed in the congregational system. I have been in more than one situation over the years where the resistors to a plan have saved us from making big mistakes and in others where resistance has led to refinements that have made the end product much better. When you meet resistance to change, it is best to stop for a moment and ask what's really going on. Even better, take the person or persons who are resisting out to coffee or lunch and listen, really listen, to their concerns. Sometimes, all they need is to be heard, and when they are, even if they don't "get their way," the chances will be greater that they will, if only begrudgingly, join the rest of the community in moving ahead.

INDIVIDUAL RESISTANCE

The reasons people resist change are many, but most tend to fall into two categories: external resistance and internal resistance. External forms of resistance come from "outside" the person who is objecting to a change and usually have to do with the process used for introducing the change to the congregation. Lack of information, questions about the implications of a change or the timing of the decision-making process, and a lack of trust in decision-makers are a few examples. Internal resistance comes from within the person who is opposed to a change. These objections can involve loss, fear, or conflicts with a person's core theology, values, or principles.

EXTERNAL RESISTANCE

Lack of information is one of the easiest forms of resistance to address. If someone feels they have insufficient knowledge about a proposed change, the needed information can be provided or sought out. I usually assume that if one or two people are missing some significant information, others will be missing it too. Rumors can kill a proposed change. Honest, consistent communication that gives everyone an opportunity to speak and be heard and promotes sharing of all available information about proposed changes often takes care of this kind of resistance.

Questions about the implications for change can be more challenging. Sometimes these are simple—like what the impact will be on the budget. Other times, the implications are fuzzier, like how a change in worship time will affect families, the elderly, or people who live farther away from the church. Perhaps the objection comes from a concern for the unintended consequences a change may produce. Some unintended consequences can be identified and addressed, but unintended consequences can never be eliminated completely. The best way to handle this form of resistance is to make sure there is an intentional process for exploring the implications of a change and uncovering as many unintended consequences as possible. As I said in chapter 11, involving the whole congregation in these discussions will help reduce the likelihood of this kind of resistance becoming a major problem.

The timing of a change can be another source of external resistance. Some people need more time than others to think about and accept something new. If someone feels there hasn't been enough time to understand the proposed change fully, perhaps a way can be found to give the group more time to deliberate. One of the purposes of having several opportunities to give and receive feedback and share thoughts in a collaborative process is to give people who need more time the opportunity to think things through. "Trial periods" before a final decision are valuable for many reasons, including giving those who are feeling this kind of resistance time to get on board. On the other hand, a congregation's delay in making a decision can also be problematic. Waiting too long to act can drain away energy and enthusiasm and frustrate early adaptors, whose entrepreneurial spirit and willingness to take risks are needed in the early days of a new venture.

Responding to those who truly believe that the proposed changes are not in the best interest of the congregation can be difficult. It is important to hear these people out. Often, they are the ones who can see problems in a plan that the leaders have missed. If there is significant resistance of this kind, it is probably best to slow down, carefully consider the concerns being raised, and either address those concerns or consider another path.

Finally, lack of trust in the system, in leaders past or present, or in the process can be deal breakers. Rebuilding trust is hard and sometimes impossible. Intentionally building cohesive relationships within the congregation and practicing good communication can establish trust from the beginning but will also go a long way to reestablishing trust that has been broken. If the leaders have done something to shatter the trust of the congregation, confession, repentance, forgiveness, and reconciliation processes may be needed to rebuild relationships. Sometimes, however, when trust is severely broken, new leadership may be called for. Replacing leaders can be very painful and bring deep and difficult grief of its own that will need to be worked through before the congregation can move forward again. But without this step, change might be impossible.

Trust is part of the glue that holds a congregational system together. Loss and grief often result in disequilibrium that sows doubt and uncertainty among the members and participants in the congregation. As we have seen, the resulting anxiety often gets focused on the leaders. If the congregation is able to work through its grief and identify and address the anxiety, trust can be restored, and resistance will diminish.

Finally, trust in God, and in God's enduring, unequivocal faithfulness, is critical to implementing any plan for a new future. Making it a priority to attend to and build on this most central relationship will permeate the whole congregation and contribute to our ability to extend our trust in God to our brothers and sisters in the community of faith.

INTERNAL RESISTANCE

Internal resistance can be difficult to get your finger on and is often tied up with the experience of loss and grief. Resistance can result when people feel they will lose something valuable because of a proposed change. This loss can be something concrete like the worship time that best fits their weekly routine, or it can be rooted in less tangible losses, such as the loss of status, a sense of belonging, or a feeling of competence and self-efficacy. A new hymnal or style of worship can bring significant resistance because of people's fear they will feel uncomfortable wrestling with the unfamiliar, such as a new order for the service or new music, for example. A new emphasis on youth ministry and young families can leave elders feeling disenfranchised. An influx of newcomers may leave longtime members with the sense that they no longer have a place in the life of the congregation. Helping members name these losses and work through the grief associated with them are the best ways to address these forms of resistance.

In my experience, the most difficult form of internal resistance in the face of change comes from conflicts between an individual's theology, values, or principles and the changes being proposed for the congregation. For example, a plan to make the congregation more inclusive of LGBTQ individuals may conflict with some members' beliefs about homosexuality. A decision to share a building with an interfaith partner may challenge a person's theology about people who do not belong to Christianity. Our theology, values, and principles form some of the deepest layers of who we are as human beings, and if we feel they are being compromised, our worldview and sense of self can be challenged, sometimes setting off powerful crises.

One way to avoid this form of resistance is to make sure that changes which will touch at people's core theology, values, and principles are studied thoroughly and carefully before any decision to implement change occurs. To proceed with a change without first addressing the potential for such fundamental concerns could shatter the congregation.

During this time of study and reflection, leaders will need to work doubly hard to make sure the whole congregation is involved in the conversation and that communication about how the concerns are being addressed is clear and regular. If the decision is made to move forward, communication about the reasons for moving in that direction will be vital to making sure everyone understands what is happening and why. If it is decided not to move forward on the grounds of theology, values, or principles, the rationale for that decision will need to be communicated as well. Even if these fundamental conflicts of theology, values, and principles are addressed in open and transparent ways, intentional work will likely need to be done to reconcile people on the different sides of the conflict (and there can be many "sides") and to address any experience of loss or grief caused by the disagreements or conflict. Finding someone from outside the congregation who is trained to facilitate such a healing process is highly recommended.

If resistance on the basis of theology, values, or principles still exists after a period of careful study and dialogue, it might be better for everyone if the congregation encourages and even helps those who are resisting to find a faith community more closely aligned with who they are and what they believe. In my opinion, this is always a last resort and should only be turned to when all other avenues toward finding common ground and reconciliation have been exhausted. Encouraging someone to leave is never easy, even if we think it is for the best. It is terribly painful for everyone involved, and divisive to the congregation.

Using a process like appreciative inquiry that involves the whole congregation and identifies the positive core of the congregation before changes are proposed and then designs new ministry and mission based on the strengths and values found in the positive core should reduce the likelihood of this kind of resistance surfacing. But it doesn't eliminate the possibility.

SYSTEMIC RESISTANCE

The forms of resistance we have been discussing are related to individual members of the congregation and the way they experience the possibility of change. This resistance needs to be handled on a one-to-one basis or by working with small groups of people who share similar concerns with the proposed changes. Frequently, however, resistance to change is more systemic. In my work with congregations facing change, I have identified four common sources of systemic resistance that need to be addressed before a congregation can move forward. My colleague Pastor Liz Albertson has organized them around four *F* words: *fear, fatigue, fondness,* and *finances.* Fear, fatigue, and fondness are all symptoms of the grief that comes from loss we have been discussing. The disruption and disequilibrium caused by loss can leave a congregation fearful of the future. Trying to address the loss of the past with technical rather than adaptive solutions can wear people out in unsuccessful attempts to re-create the past. Fondness for the way things are, in spite of the reality of loss, can actually reflect a desire for the way things used to be and result in the yearning to "change backward" discussed in chapter 11.

Finances, however, are another matter. Financial challenges in a declining congregation are not a symptom of grief and loss, but one of the losses that must be grieved and adapted to if a congregation is to embrace God's future and take up new ways of doing ministry. An apparent lack of financial resources can affect a congregation in many ways. Financial stress can limit imagination, creativity, and a willingness to risk trying new things. Declining budgets can result in a congregation's inability to pay a pastor or other staff, maintain buildings, and ultimately cover basic bills. Financial decline can lead to a congregation wrestling with the sustainability of their ministry and raise the question of whether to draw the ministry of the congregation to a close.

Adapting to financial challenges and embracing God's future with creativity will require a congregation to change how it thinks about the financial and other resources at its disposal. Moving from scarcity thinking to abundance thinking (which is different from the so-called prosperity gospel) requires a significant shift in paradigms for most congregations. Whole books have been written on making the shift from scarcity to abundance thinking, and I commend them to you.[1] Abundance thinking starts by focusing on what you have rather than what you don't have. Every congregation or ministry, no matter how small, has assets that God can use for ministry. I have seen congregations with far fewer than twenty people in worship do powerful ministry by using what God has given them. One tiny congregation I know has housed and managed the community clothing bank for years. Remember the story of St. Thomas? They had to figure out how to be a congregation of two hundred rather than a thousand. It wasn't easy. It meant selling some property, reimagining their staff, and reenergizing their volunteers. I tell our synod congregations all the time that small is not bad . . . it's just different. Jesus started his ministry with twelve guys and a handful of women, and look what they accomplished! As we begin to focus on the gifts and blessings God has placed in our hands, rather than the absence of resources, we can begin to imagine doing ministry in new ways to use what we do have more creatively for the sake of the gospel.

Creative stewardship of assets can sometimes mean letting go of some assumptions about what it means to be a church. The assumption that every church should have its own pastor is a difficult one to let go. However, through much of the history of the church and in many places today, including places like Tanzania, where the church is growing, one pastor per parish is not the norm. Three small congregations I worked with realized that by calling a pastor together, they would release funds for doing ministry in new ways. Rather than seeing this decision as a move to shore up declining ministries, they truly saw their decision as a way to do ministry more effectively. While these churches still struggle today, they are much more vibrant ministries because of their decision.

The assumption that every church should have its own building is also a hard one to give up. And yet, vital ministries all across the country and around the world meet in homes, storefronts, pubs, restaurants, schools, and many other locations. Churches like the one I described in Tanzania worship outdoors. Increasingly, congregations are sharing space with other congregations and ministries. The Arkansas-Oklahoma Synod, where I serve, shares the church building where we office with a Methodist congregation, a counselor, a theater group, and a music teacher. Because, as we have seen, our buildings are "scrapbooks of memories," giving them up can be extremely painful and result in further experiences of loss and grief that will need to be worked through. But making these hard decisions can also open us up to new and exciting opportunities to do ministry in new ways.

Finally, deciding to end a congregation's time of ministry well may be the most faithful way a congregation can embrace God's future and use its assets creatively for the sake of the gospel. Walking with a congregation that has decided to close is one of the hardest things I have to do as a bishop. But helping a congregation end well can give the congregation the opportunity to mourn together, remember its past, and give thanks for all the ways God has ministered through them. It can also allow a congregation to be a blessing for continuing ministries. The congregation's legacy can continue through gifts to ongoing ministries, opening up new possibilities for those ministries. I have seen closing congregations set up scholarships for training new pastors; share their abundance to start a new congregation; give their property for a new ministry center; endow social service ministries, seminaries, colleges, and universities of the church; and support denominational mission plans and programs. Members dispersed from a congregation that has closed carry the legacy of that congregation with them wherever they continue their personal faith journey. When a congregation closes, members lose their spiritual home. This is a significant loss for many, and careful attention must be given at the conclusion of the ministry to care for and support these members in their grief. If this is not done well, those brothers and sisters in Christ may carry unresolved grief with them for the rest of their lives. But when it is done well, these brothers and sisters can become an asset to their new congregations, bringing their gifts and skills along with the wisdom of their nostalgic memories to enrich their new spiritual homes.

In Conversation

- How do fear, fatigue, fondness, and finances get in the way of change in the life of your congregation?
- How have you addressed them?
- How might you address them in the future?
- What other sources of resistance have you faced?
- How might you walk with people who are opposed to the changes being proposed and implemented?

Working through resistance by addressing the external, internal, and systemic concerns raised by individuals and groups in the congregation can free us to make the changes necessary to embrace God's future without forgetting the past. While we may not be able to resolve all the reasons for resistance, reducing the resistance by listening carefully and responding graciously to those who have concerns can remove enough barriers for all but the most entrenched resisters to accept the changes being proposed.

Implementing creative change in the life of a congregation and taking up God's mission and ministry in new ways requires desiring that change, casting a vision drawn from the core of who we are, designing sustainable plans, and taking those all-important first steps forward into the future God is calling us to embrace. Working together and engaging the whole congregation in this process will include lovingly and respectfully working through our concerns, questions, and disagreements as brothers and sisters in Christ. In an ever-changing world, this process needs to become a way of life for our congregations and the whole church.

EMBRACING A CHANGING FUTURE

A lot has changed in the life of the church since the mid-1960s. Throughout this book, we have been looking at how working through the tasks of the grief process can help us address the ways those changes and the losses that have resulted have affected congregations as they adapt to the new realities we face and take up new ways of engaging in mission and ministry.

Because there is no sign that the pace of change in the world around us is going to slow down any day soon, this grief work will continue to be a part of congregational life for the foreseeable future. As we think about embracing God's future it is important for us to consider the trends and challenges that are likely to shape that future and how they will affect the way we carry out the ministry of the gospel as we move forward. In 2016, 2017, and 2018, the Pew Research Center released demographic studies of trends that are and will be shaping the United States and the world in the decades ahead.[2] As we come full circle in our study of loss, grief, and nostalgia in congregational life, we need to ask how these trends might set the agenda for our conversations about mission and ministry in the American context in the days ahead.

RACIAL AND ETHNIC DIVERSITY

According to the Pew report and other studies, Americans are becoming more racially and ethnically diverse. The 2016 report says that by 2055, the United States will not have a single racial or ethnic majority.[3] New immigrants are coming from the Middle East, Africa, and Asia.[4] In 2015, there were more new immigrants from Asia than from Latin America. This growing diversity is increasing in rural as well as urban and suburban communities in our country.

We need to ask how the church will adapt to that diversity. How can we learn to know neighbors who come from different cultures and traditions, and partner with them in ministry? How will these new brothers and sisters challenge and change our understanding of ourselves and the gospel of love and grace we proclaim?

THE RISE OF THE MILLENNIALS

In 2019, millennials (young adults born from 1981 to 1996) surpassed the baby boomers (born from 1946 to 1964) as the largest adult generation in the United States. Even before 2019, millennials were the largest generation in the workforce (35 percent).[5] Like each successive generation in recent memory, the millennials are different from the generations before them.[6] This is certainly true in how they think about faith and religion. Thirty-five percent of millennials do not identify with any organized religious institution.[7] Still, many millennials are interested in "spirituality" and believe in God.

How will we proclaim the gospel in this emerging context? What kind of faith community will this new generation be looking for as they grow older, and how might the church speak to their questions, concerns, and yearnings?

THE AGING WORLD

While millennials have supplanted baby boomers as the largest generation, the aging of the baby-boom generation is swelling the ranks of the retired and the number of elders in our communities. This aging of the general population is occurring not only in the United States but around the world.[8] Aging baby boomers are going to place increasing burdens on health-care systems and other services for the elderly. In my own community I have noticed a number of new facilities for "memory care" that have been built in just the past few years.

How will the church, already concerned about the aging of its members, minister to these baby boomers as they enter the last third of their lives? Perhaps, rather than attempting to re-create the days when churches were full of families and children, churches already populated by senior citizens should acknowledge that they may be uniquely suited to minister to their peers as they move into retirement and their later years. Could that be the future God is calling us to embrace?

CHANGING HOUSEHOLDS

The percentage of Americans who live in middle-class households is shrinking. In 2015, the number of US adults living in a middle-income household fell below 50 percent, and the gap between middle- and upper-income families continues to widen.[9] The structure of and relationships within families continue to change. In the 2018 study, it was reported that a record 64 million Americans are now living in multigenerational families.[10] Cohabitation, including unmarried parents raising children together, continues to increase.[11]

How will the changing economic and other realities of family life cause us to rethink the way we do ministry? How will these realities in our nation and, even more, in our local communities affect the human and financial resources for ministry? How can we respond with love and compassion to the growing needs of these neighbors who live all around us and are a part of our own families? How can we more creatively use the resources God has placed in our hands? What might we learn from previous generations who did effective ministry with considerably fewer resources than we have?

OTHER TRENDS

These are just a few of the trends we could identify as we think about the changes that will call for creative adaptation by the church in the years ahead. Shifts in weather patterns caused by climate change, the growing diversity of our religious landscape, the growth of those who have no religious affiliation, changes in employment patterns, emerging technologies, and a host of other changes will need to be attended to as we consider how to proclaim and live out the gospel message in our world.

In order to embrace God's future, congregations and church leaders will need to stay informed about these changes and continue to initiate appreciative conversations about how best to adapt to them and to address the losses and grief these changes cause both in our congregations and in the lives of individual members. Similar to change itself, our grief work is never really done. From our first experience of loss on the day of our birth to the loss of our own selves on the day of our death, we have to deal with the emotions, physical effects, behavioral impacts, and spiritual implications of the grief that comes with those losses. As we work through the experience of loss, our grief binds us for a time and then is resolved as we reclaim new energy for living.

REMEMBERING FORWARD

For a congregation mourning the loss of the past, the goal of working through the grief process is to redefine our relationship with the past so that we can step into God's future with boldness. Once we have worked through the pain of our grief, the challenges to adaptation, and our resistance to change, we can be freed to move from yearning for a return to the past to drawing on nostalgic memories for strength and wisdom. Tapping into the positive core of our congregation, we can find the courage and insight we need for doing ministry in new ways as we adapt to the changing contexts in which we find ourselves.

By living in the tension between the roots of our past and the challenges of the future—learning from the past, studying the present, and experimenting for the future—the congregation "remembers forward," constantly considering where it has been and where it is going as it dreams and designs for mission and ministry. We embrace God's future knowing that what we are doing now may not work tomorrow, and what doesn't work today may hold possibilities for ministry down the road. This remembering forward must become a way of life for congregations that want to thrive in a constantly shifting context while remaining anchored in the Way of Jesus Christ.

When I served as campus pastor at the University of South Dakota, we would always begin a new school year by having a student council planning retreat just before the start of the semester. After opening with an extended time of Bible study and prayer, the council reviewed the year that had just passed, reflecting on what worked well and what didn't. It was a great time to tell stories and reminisce about the experiences we'd shared, remember, give thanks for students who had graduated or transferred, and celebrate the contribution of the newcomers who had joined us during the year.

After we finished reflecting on the past, I would put up a blank piece of newsprint and ask, "So what is our ministry going to look like this year?" Everything was on the table . . . except worship, which was always a required part of the ministry, though how and when we worshiped was always open for discussion and change. We'd start by listing things we wanted to keep. Then we would talk about the things we wanted to let go. That was not always an easy discussion. The seniors and juniors, the "elders" of our community, often wanted to keep everything. The freshmen and sophomores were always more open to innovation and change. There was always some grief when we decided to let some things go, but to others we said, "Good riddance!"

After we listed the things we wanted to keep and those we wanted to let go, we moved to a discussion about the talents and interests of the new group of leaders. We explored how they could use their assets to do ministry in the year ahead. As we brainstormed ideas, a new ministry plan started to emerge that reflected who they were at that moment. More than once after this discussion of assets, the original "keep" list would be revised.

I remember the year we stopped doing coffeehouses. This cornerstone program of the ministry had run its course. It was a painful thing to admit. The students who started the program were long since gone, and the new generation didn't have much interest in poetry and folk music. But they did like cooking. That year, we started a weekly dinner that proved very popular. Four years later, a new group of students, who struggled to boil ramen noodles, released that program and searched for their own "thing" (though I'm not sure they ever found it). Their "thing" was not to have a "thing." They did a broad variety of programs and activities during that year rather than settling on a more fixed routine.

I have always said that a campus ministry, where a "generation" is four or five years long, is like a condensed time-lapse movie of a congregation's much longer generational life. With the constant turnover of students, things change quickly on a campus. That means the ebb and flow of growth and decline, the birth and death of ministries and programs, the experience of loss and grief, and the emergence of new life happen more quickly. These patterns are easier to recognize and understand. Adapting to change and trying new things is an everyday part of ministry. Over the years, I learned that just because a ministry or program worked during one school year didn't mean it would have success in the next one. In the same way, something that failed to get traction one year could take off when a new school year began.

I introduced similar annual review retreats in the congregations where I served. While the dynamics were much different and the status quo more established, the process of review, evaluation, and reimagination still gave us a built-in opportunity to connect the past with the present and give us vision for the future. Because the congregations were much larger than the small campus communities where I served, the discussion about how to allow ministries to flow from assets was more complex but still helpful in sparking creativity and new ideas. Change came more slowly in the congregation, but it was still a reality we were aware of and considered as we put together our plans for the year ahead.

In both campus communities and congregations, as we remembered forward, we affirmed how God had been at work among us in the year that had passed and used that awareness to give us confidence and assurance that God would continue leading us as we thought about the future. As we studied the stories of Scripture, we could see how our experience of God's faithfulness and steadfastness reflected the experience of God's people down through the ages.

In Conversation

Take newsprint and list all the ministries, programs, and activities in your congregation you can think of.

- Put a check mark by the ones you think should be continued, an *x* by those that have clearly run their course or need a significant overhaul, and a question mark by those you're not sure of.

- Where do you see God at work in the ministries, programs, and activities you listed? Consider the guidance of the Holy Spirit in the ministries you see continuing, ending, or in need of an overhaul.

- Reflect on what your lists say about the ministry of your congregation, what might need to be grieved, and the changes you may need to consider as you embrace God's future for your community of faith.

- After your conversation, discuss how you might have this kind of conversation in a healthy way with your whole congregation.

Vital, creative congregations of any size have a clear sense of their history, their present story, their gifts and assets, and the context in which they are called to do ministry. They possess a deep passion for sharing the good news of Jesus's life, death, and resurrection and for serving the ever-changing world around them in Jesus's name. They are aware that the world around them is constantly changing and that they always need to be about the business of adapting their ministry to embody the good news of Jesus Christ in new ways. Vital congregations know they need to be open to change, while always remaining deeply rooted in their positive core values, strengths, and wisdom. They understand the need to remember forward, not backward, as they learn from the past and step into the future God is calling them to embrace.

Being an ever-changing church in an ever-changing world means we are always looking for new ways to tell the old, old story of Jesus and his love. This can be challenging work, often involving loss and grief. But we do not ever face this journey on our own. God is always at work

248

among us, calling us into the future that God is always creating. Paul tells the Corinthians that in Christ, they are a new creation—that what is old has passed away and everything has become new. Reconciled to God, the church through the ages has been called to be ambassadors for Christ in a changing world, to share God's love and grace through ministries of proclamation and service. Today, God is still bringing new life to Christ's church. Embracing God's future means being open to the work God has always done—making us new creations through Jesus Christ our Lord.

BIBLE STUDY: 2 CORINTHIANS 5:17-21

1. Read 2 Corinthians 5:17–21.

2. Discuss the following questions:

- Where are there signs of God's new creation in your congregation?

- How can you nurture, support, and encourage these signs of life? If you can't think of any, how might you work together in new ways to discover the life that is there? (It's there because God is there!)

3. Read Matthew 13:44–53.

4. Reflect on or discuss these questions:

- The three parables in Matthew 13:44–50 describe the kingdom of heaven. What do you think Jesus is trying to teach us about the kingdom? What don't you understand?

- Which of the three parables speaks most directly to you? Your congregation? Your context for ministry? Why?

Postlude: A Changing Church in a Changing World

And the one who was seated on the throne said, "See, I am making all things new." (Rev 21:5)

"Hey! Pastor Girlinghouse!" Carrie shouted at me from across the quad. I hadn't seen her since she handed in her final exam two semesters earlier. She jogged across the broad grassy boulevard to the sidewalk where I was standing, smiling broadly. "I just wanted to tell you how much better I'm doing," she said, a little out of breath.

Carrie had been a student in my "Death: Grief and Growth" class at the university. An engineering student, she took the class as an elective because she was struggling with her grief over the sudden death of her older sister. She rarely made it through class without getting tears in her eyes. After class, she often followed me out into the hall, down the stairs, and across the quad, pouring out her grief, wrestling with her questions, trying to figure out how she could go on without a sibling who had been her best friend, protector, and hero.

"You told me it would get better, and, I have to admit, I didn't believe you. I wanted her back so bad. It wasn't easy. It was terrible. But you were right, it did get better. Oh, I still

251

have my hard days now and then, but I know Cindy would have wanted me to go on with my life. I guess that's what I'm doing. I think she'd be happy with how far I've come."

Through these pages, we have been walking together through the twisted, often difficult journey we call "grief." Our conversations have traveled through the rough terrain of loss, the pain it generates, and the adjustments it demands. Unlikely heroes on an unwanted quest, we have worked through the tasks grief presents and confronted the challenges it raises, overcoming them and then circling around and overcoming them again. We have encountered our past, redefined our relationship with it, drawn strength from it, and learned how to use our nostalgic memories as launching points for embracing the future God intends for us.

Like Carrie's grief for her sister, the process hasn't always been easy. The temptation to hang onto the past, to re-create it, is great. It's equally tempting to ignore our grief, swallow it, and listen to our culture's urging to forget the past and get on with life. But we have learned from hard experience that the only way through grief is to grieve. The only way forward is to remember the past and find a way to carry it with us, even as we make the adjustments and changes necessary to live in a new way.

THE MYTH OF THE UNCHANGING CHURCH

Throughout the book we have talked about change—the change that comes as a result of loss, the changes that come to us from forces that are often beyond our control, and those we choose to make as we embrace God's future and imagine doing ministry in new ways. We have considered the implications of the paradox that the presence of change in our lives is the one thing that doesn't change.

Because all things change, the myth that the church is the one place in life that doesn't or shouldn't change is just that, a myth. Since the day Jesus called the first disciples to leave their fishing nets along the Sea of Galilee, followers of Jesus have experienced change after change, loss after loss, and death after death as we have lived out the gospel and proclaimed it to the world in word and deed. But in the light of Easter's empty tomb, we also know that life follows death, and new life can grow from experiences of loss and grief.

Since the day Jesus sent his disciples out into the world, the world around us has changed—sometimes for the worse, sometimes for the better. As nations and empires have risen and fallen around us, the church of Jesus Christ has adapted. The church has survived wars and plagues; persecutions and tyrants; famine, storm, and cultural upheaval; and its own shortsighted policies, destructive violence, and abusive acts. Through it all, the good news of God's love and grace has persisted and changed lives for the better. That story alone should assure us that God will walk with us through all the changes, loss, and grief we face today.

REMEMBERING THE PAST AS WE EMBRACE GOD'S FUTURE

As we remember the stories of God's steadfast love and unwavering faithfulness, we are strengthened and encouraged by God's promise to walk with us through the valley of the shadow of death and to make all things new in Jesus Christ. As we pass through our grief at the loss of what used to be, we are strengthened by the Holy Spirit to embrace what is yet to come, knowing that the fullness of God's reign always lies in front of us, not behind. Loss can lead to growth and new insights into what it means to be children of God and God's ambassadors of reconciliation in an ever-changing world.

The church of Jesus Christ will continue to change. That is guaranteed. Congregations and denominations will rise and fall over time, just as they always have. But I am convinced, absolutely convinced, that God is not done with God's church. Not yet. God will continue to empower God's church to continue the mission of the gospel, even if that's in unexpected and seemingly unorthodox ways. As we partner with God in this mission, we will continue to fall short, to make mistakes, wrong turns, and bad decisions. Forgiveness will be needed. But sometimes in spite of ourselves, the love and grace of God will continue to be shared, change lives, and give life.

So, as we come to the end of this journey, it is my prayer for you and your congregation that remembering forward, you will come to know the power of God's love and grace accompanying you as you face changes in your community, grieve your losses, draw strength and encouragement from your nostalgic memories, and embrace with boldness and humility the future that God is, even now, creating for you.

The Rev. Michael K. Girlinghouse
Epiphany 2019

Notes

PART I: LEAVING EDEN: AN INTRODUCTION TO LOSS, GRIEF, AND NOSTALGIA

1. Unless otherwise noted, the stories and illustrations I use in the book are compilations of experiences I have had in life and ministry. All the names, as well as other identifiable details, have been changed.

2. Erica G. Hepper et al., "Pancultural Nostalgia: Prototypical Conceptions across Cultures," *Emotion* 2014 August 14, no. 4 (2014): 733–47, https://doi.org/10.1037/a0036790.

CHAPTER 1: EMPTY PLACES: THE EXPERIENCE OF LOSS

1. Charles A. Corr et al., *Death and Dying, Life and Living*, 4th ed. (Belmont, CA: Wadsworth/Thomson Learning, 2003), 208–9.

2. We'll discuss the experience of grief in detail in chap. 2.

3. Therese A. Rando, *Grief, Dying and Death: Clinical Interventions for Caregivers* (Champaign, IL: Research Press, 1984), 16–18.

CHAPTER 2: A TWISTING ROAD: THE JOURNEY OF GRIEF

1. Charles A. Corr et al., *Death and Dying, Life and Living*, 4th ed. (Belmont, CA: Wadsworth/Thomson Learning, 2003), 210–11.

2. Samuel J. Marwit and Dennis Klass, "Grief and the Inner Representation of the Deceased," in Dennis Klass et al., eds., *Continuing Bonds: New Understandings of Grief* (Bristol, PA: Taylor & Francis, 1996), 298.

3. This quote is widely attributed to Margaret Mead in a variety of websites, articles, and publications. See AZ Quotes, http://tinyurl.com/y5pdzz8a.

4. Elisabeth Kübler-Ross, *On Death and Dying: What the Dying Have to Teach Doctors, Nurses, Clergy and Their Own Families* (New York: Simon & Schuster/Collier, 1970).

5. Kübler-Ross, *On Death and Dying*.

6. Therese A. Rando, *Treatment of Complicated Mourning* (Champaign, IL: Research Press, 1993), 44–60.

7. Sigmund Freud, "Mourning and Melancholia" (1917), in *Collected Papers* (London: Hogarth, 1948), 4:152–70, http://tinyurl.com/y5yvl75r.

8. Dennis Klass et al., eds., *Continuing Bonds: New Understandings of Grief* (Bristol, PA: Taylor & Francis, 1996).

9. J. William Worden, *Grief Counseling and Grief Therapy: A Handbook for the Mental Health Practitioner*, 4th ed. (New York: Springer, 2009), iii.

10. Worden, *Grief Counseling and Grief Therapy*, 39–52.

11. Rando, *Complicated Mourning*, 44.

12. Worden, *Grief Counseling and Grief Therapy*, 46–49.

13. Worden, *Grief Counseling and Grief Therapy*, 47.

14. Ronnie Janoff-Bulman, *Shattered Assumptions: Towards*

a New Psychology of Trauma (New York: Free Press, 1992), http://tinyurl.com/yyhaggu7.

15. Phyllis R. Silverman and Steven L. Nickman, "Concluding Thoughts," in Klass et al., *Continuing Bonds*, 351.

16. Samuel J. Marwit and Dennis Klass, "Grief and the Inner Representation of the Deceased," in Klass et al., *Continuing Bonds*, 298.

CHAPTER 3: A CLOUD OF WITNESSES: NOSTALGIA, YEARNING, AND THE PAST

1. Clay Routledge, *Nostalgia: A Psychological Resource* (New York: Taylor & Francis, 2016), 23.

2. Routledge, *Nostalgia*, 3.

3. Constantine Sedikides and Tim Wildschut, "Past Forward: Nostalgia as a Motivational Force," *Trends in Cognitive Sciences* 20, no. 5 (2016): 8.

4. Sedikides and Wildschut, "Past Forward," 3.

5. Routledge, *Nostalgia*, 51–68.

6. Routledge, *Nostalgia*, 75.

7. "International Classification of Diseases, 11th Revision," World Health Organization, 2018, http://tinyurl.com/y4kkapku.

8. Alexander H. Jordan and Brett T. Litz, "Prolonged Grief Disorder: Diagnostic, Assessment, and Treatment Considerations," *Professional Psychology: Research and Practice* 45, no. 3 (2014): 181, http://dx.doi.org/10.1037/a0036836.

9. Jordan and Litz, "Prolonged Grief Disorder," 182.

CHAPTER 4: THE STORY OF LOSS: MINISTRY IN A WORLD OF CHANGE

1. J. William Worden, *Grief Counseling and Grief Therapy: A Handbook for the Mental Health Practitioner*, 4th ed. (New York: Springer, 2009), 39, 42.

2. Therese A. Rando, *Treatment of Complicated Mourning* (Champaign, IL: Research Press, 1993), 44.

3. Peter L. Steinke, *How Your Church Family Works: Understanding Congregations as Emotional Systems* (Lanham, MD: Rowman & Littlefield, 2006), Kindle loc 6.

4. Robert D. Putnam, *Bowling Alone: The Collapse and Revival of American Community* (New York: Simon and Schuster, 2000).

5. Putnam, *Bowling Alone*, 280.

6. Putnam, *Bowling Alone*, 188.

7. Kenneth W. Inskeep, "Priorities in Context: Sustainability and Membership Growth—A Background Paper for the Future Directions Table" (Chicago: Evangelical Lutheran Church in America, 2016).

8. "ELCA Facts," Evangelical Lutheran Church in America, https://tinyurl.com/yxzfwjwd.

9. "Religious Landscape Survey," Pew Research Center, 2016, http://tinyurl.com/yxcargs4, and Frank Newport, "Five Key Findings on Religion in the US," Gallup News, December 23, 2016, http://tinyurl.com/y5y4kf5f.

10. Newport, "Five Key Findings."

11. Putnam, *Bowling Alone*, 184. Quoting Robert Wuthnow, *Sharing the Journey* (New York: Free Press 1994), 6.

12. Putnam, *Bowing Alone*, 184.

13. David A. Roozen, "American Congregations 2015: Thriving and Surviving" (Hartford Seminary, Hartford Institute for Religion Research, 2016), 14, http://tinyurl.com/y5md3ms4.

14. Frank Newport, "Most Americans Still Believe in God," Gallup News, June 29, 2016, https://tinyurl.com/y6r7jmgw.

15. Rando, *Treatment of Complicated Mourning*, 44.

16. Steinke, *How Your Church Family Works*, 6–9.

17. Avery D. Wiseman, *On Dying and Denying* (New York: Aronson, 1972), cited in Worden, *Grief Counseling and Grief Therapy*, 43.

18. Edwin H. Friedman, *Generation to Generation: Family Process in Church and Synagogue* (New York: Guilford, 1985).

19. Michael E. Kerr, *One Family's Story: A Primer on Bowen Theory* (The Bowen Center for the Study of the Family, 2000), http://tinyurl.com/y3gh5jmf.

20. For more information on families as emotional systems, see Murray Bowen, *Family Therapy in Clinical Practice* (Lanham, MD: Rowman & Littlefield, 1978).

21. Steinke, *How Your Church Family Works*, xiii.

22. Steinke, *How Your Church Family Works*, xiv.

23. Lynne Ann DeSpelder and Albert Lee Strickland, *The Last Dance: Encountering Death and Dying, Eighth Edition* (New York: McGraw-Hill, 2009), 388–89.

24. Susan K. Gilmore and Patrick W. Fraleigh, *The Friendly Style Profile: A Guide through Calm and Storm for People at Work* (Eugene, OR: Friendly Press, 2004).

25. *Palliative care* is care for people with life-limiting illnesses that focuses on providing relief from symptoms, pain, and physical and mental stress rather than curative treatments and therapies.

26. David W. Kissane and Sidney Bloch, *Family Focused Grief Therapy* (Buckingham, UK: Open University Press, 2002).

27. Kissane and Bloch, *Family Focused Grief Therapy*, 1.

28. Kissane and Bloch, *Family Focused Grief Therapy*, 33.

29. Kissane and Bloch, *Family Focused Grief Therapy*, 33.

30. I will have a lot more to say about the role anxiety plays in a congregation's grief process in the next chapter.

31. Kissane and Bloch, *Family Focused Grief Therapy*, 16–17.

32. Kissane and Bloch, *Family Focused Grief Therapy*, 33.

33. Kissane and Bloch, *Family Focused Grief Therapy*, 33.

34. Kissane and Bloch, *Family Focused Grief Therapy*, 36.

35. Roozen, "American Congregations 2015," 5.

CHAPTER 5: A SCRAPBOOK OF MEMORIES: THE GRIEF RESPONSE

1. Therese A. Rando, *Treatment of Complicated Mourning* (Champaign, IL: Research Press, 1993), 44.

2. Peter L. Steinke, *How Your Church Family Works: Understanding Congregations as Emotional Systems* (Lanham, MD: Rowman & Littlefield, 2006), 9.

3. Steinke, *How Your Church Family Works*, 9.

4. J. William Worden, *Grief Counseling and Grief Therapy: A Handbook for the Mental Health Practitioner*, 4th ed. (New York: Springer, 2009), 43.

5. Edwin H. Friedman, *Generation to Generation: Family Process in Church and Synagogue* (New York: Guilford, 1985), 129–32.

6. Steinke, *How Your Church Family Works*, preface.

7. Steinke, *How Your Church Family Works*, 15.

8. Steinke, *How Your Church Family Works*, 16.

9. Steinke, *How Your Church Family Works*, 25–26.

10. Therese A. Rando, *Grief, Dying and Death: Clinical Interventions for Caregivers* (Champaign, IL: Research Press, 1984), 34.

11. Steinke, *How Your Church Family Works*, 9.

12. Worden, *Grief Counseling and Grief Therapy*, 243.

CHAPTER 6: A WELL OF TEARS: EXPRESSING OUR GRIEF

1. Therese A. Rando, *Treatment of Complicated Mourning* (Champaign, IL: Research Press, 1993), 401.

2. David W. Kissane and Sidney Bloch, *Family Focused Grief Therapy* (Buckingham, UK: Open University Press, 2002), 95–96.

3. Psalms of lament include 5, 10, 13, 22, 28, 42, 44, 55, 57, 60, 74, 77, 80, 85, 86, 90, 123, 126, 142.

4. "Filters" refers to how we take in new information and interpret it according to prior experiences, perspectives, and cultural norms.

5. Mothers Against Drunk Driving, https://tinyurl.com/y6qv6lu9.

6. Kansas City Hospice, https://tinyurl.com/yy97ndft.

7. Wanda Kelsey-Mendez, ed., "Hanging on at Holiday Time," *Journeys: A Newsletter from Grief Support Services at Kansas City Hospice & Palliative Care*, fall/winter 2014, http://tinyurl.com/y39dscze.

8. Rando, *Treatment of Complicated Mourning*, 317.

9. Rando, *Treatment of Complicated Mourning*, 319.

10. Rando, *Treatment of Complicated Mourning*, 322.

PART 3: OPENING THE BLINDS: ADAPTING TO LOSS WITHOUT FORGETTING THE PAST

1. J. William Worden, *Grief Counseling and Grief Therapy: A Handbook for the Mental Health Practitioner*, 4th ed. (New York: Springer, 2009), 46.

CHAPTER 7: AN OLD STORY IN A NEW KEY: THE ROOTS OF ADAPTIVE CHANGE

1. David W. Kissane and Sidney Bloch, *Family Focused Grief Therapy* (Buckingham, UK: Open University Press, 2002), 1. See the discussion in chap. 4.

2. Ronald A. Heifetz and Marty Linsky, *Leadership on the Line: Staying Alive through the Dangers of Leading* (Boston: Harvard Business School Press, 2002), referenced in Mark Lau Branson, *Memories, Hopes, and Conversations*, vol. 2, *Appreciative Inquiry, Missional Engagement, and Congregational Change*, 2nd ed. (Lanham, MD: Rowman & Littlefield, 2016), 32.

3. Ronald A. Heifetz, *Leadership without Easy Answers* (Cambridge, MA: Belknap Press of Harvard University Press, 1994), 87.

4. Heifetz and Linsky, *Leadership on the Line*, referenced in Branson, *Appreciative Inquiry*, 32.

5. Worden, *Grief Counseling and Grief Therapy*, 49. Worden describes a similar response in individuals experiencing grief.

6. Martha Grace Reese, *Unbinding the Gospel: Real Life Evangelism,* 2nd ed. (St. Louis: Chalice, 2008), 43.

CHAPTER 8: BEING WHO WE ARE: ADAPTIVE CHANGE AND NOSTALGIA

1. Clay Routledge, *Nostalgia: A Psychological Resource* (New York: Taylor & Francis, 2016), 52.

2. For more on this particular metaphor, see Bob Farr, *Renovate or Die: Ten Ways to Focus Your Church on Mission* (Nashville: Abingdon, 2011).

3. Curtis S. Dunkel, "The Relation Between Self-Continu-

ity and Measures of Identity," *Identity* 5, no. 1 (2005): 21–34, DOI: https://doi.org/10.1207/s1532706xid0501_2.

4. Routledge, *Nostalgia*, 76.

5. Routledge, *Nostalgia*, 78.

6. Routledge, *Nostalgia*, 51–68.

7. Routledge, *Nostalgia*, 53.

8. Routledge, *Nostalgia*, 63.

9. Routledge, *Nostalgia*, 61, 63.

10. David Cooperrider and Diana D. Whitney, *Appreciative Inquiry: A Positive Revolution in Change* (San Francisco: Berrett-Koehler, 2005), 8.

11. A detailed description of the process of appreciative inquiry is beyond the scope of this book. For a fuller treatment of this process, I recommend you consult Cooperrider and Whitney, *Appreciative Inquiry*; Mark Lau Branson, *Memories, Hopes, and Conversations*, vol. 2, *Appreciative Inquiry, Missional Engagement, and Congregational Change*, 2nd ed. (Lanham, MD: Rowman & Littlefield, 2016); or Jane Magruder Watkins et al., *Appreciative Inquiry: Change at the Speed of Imagination*, 2nd ed. (San Francisco: Pfeiffer, 2011), among others.

12. Cooperrider and Whitney, *Appreciative Inquiry*, 9.

13. Cooperrider and Whitney, *Appreciative Inquiry*, 15–17.

14. Cooperrider and Whitney, *Appreciative Inquiry*, 25.

15. Cooperrider and Whitney, *Appreciative Inquiry*, 13.

CHAPTER 9: A PLACE AT THE TABLE: OVERCOMING CHALLENGES TO ADAPTIVE CHANGE

1. Wesley Grandberg-Michaelson, *Future Faith: Ten Challenges Reshaping Christianity in the 21st Century* (Minneapolis: Fortress Press, 2018).

2. David W. Kissane and Sidney Bloch, *Family Focused Grief Therapy* (Buckingham, UK: Open University Press, 2002), 97.

3. Kissane and Bloch, *Family Focused Grief Therapy*, 68–70.

4. Use Google or another search engine to search "Simple Group Building Exercises" or "Team Building Exercises."

5. Roger Fisher and William Ury, *Getting to Yes: Negotiating Agreement without Giving In*, 2nd ed. (New York: Penguin, 1991), 63.

6. Fisher and Ury, *Getting to Yes*, 58–81.

7. The Lombard Mennonite Peace Center provides excellent training in conflict transformation. See https://lmpeacecenter.org.

8. Alan Roxburgh, *Missional Map-Making* (San Francisco: Jossey-Bass, 2010), 168, referenced in Mark Lau Branson, *Memories, Hopes, and Conversations*, vol. 2, *Appreciative Inquiry, Missional Engagement, and Congregational Change*, 2nd ed. (Lanham, MD: Rowman & Littlefield, 2016), 27.

CHAPTER 10: A NEW JOURNEY: TAKING UP LIFE AGAIN

1. J. William Worden, *Grief Counseling and Grief Therapy: A Handbook for the Mental Health Practitioner*, 4th ed. (New York: Springer, 2009), 50.

2. Phyllis R. Silverman and Steven L. Nickman, "Concluding Thoughts," in *Continuing Bonds: New Understandings of Grief*, ed. Dennis Klass et al. (Bristol, PA: Taylor & Francis, 1996), 352.

3. Worden, *Grief Counseling and Grief Therapy*, 51–52.

4. Stephanie S. Gardner, "An Overview of the Skin," WebMD, July 2, 2018, https://tinyurl.com/y3g4wrkr.

5. Worden, *Grief Counseling and Grief Therapy*, 52.

6. Worden, *Grief Counseling and Grief Therapy*, 53.

7. Michael Michalko, *Cracking Creativity: The Secrets of Creative Genius* (New York: Ten Speed Press, 2001), loc. 2811, Kindle.

8. Michalko, *Cracking Creativity*, loc. 1404, Kindle.

9. Dr. Jonathan Strandjord, private conversation.

CHAPTER 11: A FORMULA FOR CHANGE: STEPPING INTO GOD'S FUTURE

1. Steven H. Cady et al., "The Change Formula: Myth, Legend or Lore?," *OD Practitioner* 46, no. 3 (2014): http://tinyurl.com/y5xmsz3l.

2. Kenneth W. Inskeep and Daniel Taylor, "Arkansas-Oklahoma Congregations and the U.S. Congregation Life Survey," January 2011.

3. Cady et al., "The Change Formula," 35–36.

4. Cady et al., "The Change Formula," 35–36.

5. Cady et al., "The Change Formula," 33–34.

6. David Cooperrider and Diana D. Whitney, *Appreciative Inquiry: A Positive Revolution in Change* (San Francisco: Berrett-Koehler, 2005), 15.

7. Cooperrider and Whitney, *Appreciative Inquiry*, 16, 27, 39.

8. Mark Lau Branson, *Memories, Hopes, and Conversations*, vol. 2, *Appreciative Inquiry, Missional Engagement, and Congregational Change*, 2nd ed. (Lanham, MD: Rowman & Littlefield, 2016), 88, 90.

9. Lao Tzu, *Tao De Ching*, trans. D. C. Lau (Harmondsworth, UK: Penguin, 1963), chap. 64.

10. Cooperrider and Whitney, *Appreciative Inquiry*, 16.

11. Branson, *Appreciative Inquiry*, 98, Kindle.

12. A more detailed process for developing provocative proposals along with examples of these proposals can be found in Branson, *Appreciative Inquiry*, 95–109.

13. Cady et al., "The Change Formula," 36.

14. David W. Kissane and Sidney Bloch, *Family Focused Grief Therapy* (Buckingham, UK: Open University Press, 2002), 72.

15. Cooperrider and Whitney, *Appreciative Inquiry*, 34.

16. Branson, *Appreciative Inquiry*, 113–15.

17. Cooperrider and Whitney, *Appreciative Inquiry*, 16.

CHAPTER 12: A NEW CREATION: EMBRACING GOD'S FUTURE

1. A great little book on asset-based ministry is Bob Sitze, *The Great Permission: An Asset-Based Field Guide for Congregations* (Chicago: Evangelical Lutheran Church in America, 2002).

2. Anthony Cilluffo and D'Vera Cohn, "7 Demographic Trends Shaping the U.S. and the World in 2018," *Pew Research FactTank: News in the Numbers*, April 25, 2018, http://tinyurl.com/y374afh9; Anthony Cilluffo and D'Vera Cohn, "10 Demographic Trends Shaping the U.S. and the World in 2017," *Pew Research FactTank: News in the Numbers*, April 27, 2017, https://tinyurl.com/yxsxo265; D'Vera Cohn and Andrea Caumont, "10 Demographic Trends That Are Shaping the U.S. and the World," *Pew Research FactTank: News in the Numbers*, March 31, 2018, http://tinyurl.com/y384flgu.

3. Cohn and Caumont, "10 Demographic Trends."

4. Cilluffo and Cohn, "7 Demographic Trends."

5. Cilluffo and Cohn, "7 Demographic Trends."

6. Cohn and Caumont, "10 Demographic Trends."

7. Cohn and Caumont, "10 Demographic Trends."

8. Cohn and Caumont, "10 Demographic Trends."
9. Cohn and Caumont, "10 Demographic Trends."
10. Cilluffo and Cohn, "7 Demographic Trends."
11. Cilluffo and Cohn, "7 Demographic Trends."

Bibliography

Bowen, Murray. *Family Therapy in Clinical Practice*. Lanham, MD: Rowman & Littlefield, 1978.

Branson, Mark Lau. *Memories, Hopes, and Conversations*. Vol. 2, *Appreciative Inquiry, Missional Engagement, and Congregational Change*. Lanham, MD: Rowman & Littlefield, 2016.

Cady, Steven H., et al. "The Change Formula: Myth, Legend, or Lore?" *OD Practitioner* 46, no. 3 (2014): http://tinyurl.com/y5xmsz3l.

Cilluffo, Anthony, and D'Vera Cohn. "7 Demographic Trends Shaping the U.S. and the World in 2018." *Pew Research FactTank: News in the Numbers*, April 25, 2018, http://tinyurl.com/y374afh9.

———. "10 Demographic Trends Shaping the U.S. and the World in 2017." *Pew Research FactTank: News in the Numbers*, April 27, 2017, https://tinyurl.com/yxsxo265.

Cohn, D'Vera, and Andrea Caumont. "10 Demographic Trends That Are Shaping the U.S. and the World." *Pew Research FactTank: News in the Numbers*, March 31, 2018, http://tinyurl.com/y384flgu.

Cooperrider, David, and Diana D. Whitney. *Appreciative Inquiry: A Positive Revolution in Change*. San Francisco: Berrett-Koehler, 2005.

Corr, Charles A., et al. *Death and Dying, Life and Living.* 4th ed. Belmont, CA: Wadsworth/Thomson Learning, 2003.

DeSpelder, Lynne Ann, and Albert Lee Strickland. *The Last Dance: Encountering Death and Dying.* 8th ed. New York: McGraw-Hill, 2009.

Dunkel, Curtis S. "The Relation between Self-Continuity and Measures of Identity." *Identity* 5, no. 1 (2005): 21–34. DOI: https://doi.org/10.1207/s1532706xid0501_2.

"ELCA Facts." Evangelical Lutheran Church in America. https://tinyurl.com/yxzfwjwd.

Fisher, Roger, and William Ury. *Getting to Yes: Negotiating Agreement without Giving In.* 2nd ed. New York: Penguin, 1991.

Friedman, Edwin H. *Generation to Generation: Family Process in Church and Synagogue.* New York: Guilford, 1985.

Freud, Sigmund. "Mourning and Melancholia" (1917). In *Collected Papers.* London: Hogarth, 1948, 4:152–70. http://tinyurl.com/y5yvl75r.

Gardner, Stephanie S. "An Overview of the Skin." WebMD, July 2, 2018, https://tinyurl.com/y3g4wrkr.

Gilmore, Susan K., and Patrick W. Fraleigh. *The Friendly Style Profile: A Guide through Calm and Storm for People at Work.* Eugene, OR: Friendly Press, 2004.

Granberg-Michaelson, Wesley. *Future Faith: Ten Challenges Reshaping Christianity in the 21st Century.* Minneapolis: Fortress Press, 2018.

Heifetz, Ronald A., and Marty Linsky. *Leadership on the Line: Staying Alive through the Dangers of Leading.* Boston: Harvard Business School Press, 2002.

Heifetz, Ronald A. *Leadership without Easy Answers*, Cambridge, MA: The Belknap Press of Harvard University Press, 1994.

Hepper, Erica G., et al. "Pancultural Nostalgia: Prototypical Conceptions Across Cultures." *Emotion* 14, no. 4 (2014): 733–47. https://doi.org/10.1037/a0036790.

Inskeep, Kenneth W., and Daniel Taylor. "Arkansas-Oklahoma Congregations and the U.S. Congregation Life Survey." January 2011.

Inskeep, Kenneth W. "Priorities in Context: Sustainability and Membership Growth; A Background Paper for the Future Directions Table." Chicago: Evangelical Lutheran Church in America, 2016.

"International Classification of Diseases, 11th Revision." World Health Organization, 2018, http://tinyurl.com/y4kkapku.

Janoff-Bulman, Ronnie. *Shattered Assumptions: Towards a New Psychology of Trauma*. New York: Free Press, 1992. http://tinyurl.com/yyhaggu7.

Jordan, Alexander H., and Brett T. Litz. "Prolonged Grief Disorder: Diagnostic, Assessment, and Treatment Considerations." *Professional Psychology: Research and Practice* 45, no. 3 (2014): 180–87. DOI: http://dx.doi.org/10.1037/a0036836.

Kelsey-Mendez, Wanda, ed. "Hanging on at Holiday Time." *Journeys: A Newsletter from Grief Support Services at Kansas City Hospice & Palliative Care*. fall/winter 2014, http://tinyurl.com/y39dscze.

Kerr, Michael E. *One Family's Story: A Primer on Bowen Theory*. The Bowen Center for the Study of the Family, 2000. http://tinyurl.com/y3gh5jmf.

Kissane, David W., and Sidney Bloch. *Family Focused Grief Therapy*. Buckingham, UK: Open University Press, 2002.

Klass, Dennis, et al. eds. *Continuing Bonds: New Understandings of Grief*. Bristol, PA: Taylor & Francis, 1996.

Koth, Jessica, and Cecelia Heffron. "Cremation on the Rise: NFDA Predicts the National Cremation Rate Will Climb a Third Within 20 Years." *National Funeral Directors Association News Releases*, July 12, 2018, http://tinyurl.com/y3z27kwf.

Kübler-Ross, Elisabeth. *On Death and Dying: What the Dying Have to Teach Doctors, Nurses, Clergy and Their Own Families*. New York: Simon & Schuster/Collier, 1970.

Michalko, Michael. *Cracking Creativity: The Secrets of Creative Genius*. New York: Ten Speed Press, 2001. Kindle.

Newport, Frank. "Five Key Findings on Religion in the US." Gallup News, December 23, 2016, http://tinyurl.com/y5y4kf5f.

———. "Most Americans Still Believe in God." Gallup News, June 29, 2016, https://tinyurl.com/y6r7jmgw.

Putnam, Robert D. *Bowling Alone: The Collapse and Revival of American Community*. New York: Simon and Schuster, 2000.

Rando, Therese A. *Grief, Dying and Death: Clinical Interventions for Caregivers*. Champaign, IL: Research Press, 1984.

———. *Treatment of Complicated Mourning*. Champaign, IL: Research Press, 1993.

Reese, Martha Grace. *Unbinding the Gospel: Real Life Evangelism*. 2nd ed. St. Louis: Chalice, 2008.

"Religious Landscape Survey." Pew Research Center, 2016, http://tinyurl.com/yxcargs4.

Roozen, David A. "American Congregations 2015: Thriving and Surviving." Hartford Seminary, Hartford Institute for Religion Research, 2016, http://tinyurl.com/y5md3ms4.

Roxburgh, Alan. *Missional Map-Making*. San Francisco: Jossey-Bass, 2010.

Routledge, Clay. *Nostalgia: A Psychological Resource*. New York: Taylor & Francis, 2016.

Sedikides, Constantine, and Tim Wildschut. "Past Forward: Nostalgia as a Motivational Force." *Trends in Cognitive Sciences* 20, no. 5 (2016): 319–21.

Steinke, Peter L. *How Your Church Family Works: Understanding Congregations as Emotional Systems*. Herndon, VA: Alban Institute, 2006.

Watkins, Jane Magruder, et al. *Appreciative Inquiry: Change at the Speed of Imagination*. 2nd ed. San Francisco: Pfeiffer, 2011.

Worden, J. William. *Grief Counseling and Grief Therapy: A Handbook for the Mental Health Practitioner.* 4th ed. New York: Springer, 2009.